ROOTS OF AGGRESSION

Consulting Editors

The Editor

LEONARD BERKOWITZ is Professor
and Chairman of the Department of Psychology
at the University of Wisconsin. He was awarded
his doctorate by the University of Michigan. He
has been a visiting professor at Stanford and
Cornell Universities and has spent a year at Oxford University under a grant from the National
Science Foundation. Professor Berkowitz was a
research psychologist for the United States Air
Force as well as a member of the Behavioral
Sciences Review Panel of the Career Development
Branch of the National Institutes of Health. Now
an associate editor of the *Journal of Personality
and Social Psychology*, he is also editing a series
entitled *Advances in Experimental Social Psychology*. During 1967–68 Professor Berkowitz served
as a consultant to President Johnson's Commis-
sion on the Causes and Prevention of Violence
and to the New York State Joint Legislative Com-
mission on Crime. He is the author of *Aggression:
A Social Psychological Analysis* (1962) and *The
Development of Motives and Values in Children*
(1964) and has written many articles for pro-
fessional journals.

ROOTS OF

EDITED BY

AGGRESSION

A RE-EXAMINATION OF THE
FRUSTRATION-AGGRESSION HYPOTHESIS

Leonard Berkowitz

ATHERTON PRESS

New York 1969

Contents

1 : *The Frustration-Aggression Hypothesis Revisited*

LEONARD BERKOWITZ

Now and then in the social sciences a theoretical proposition becomes a focal point of widespread controversy. Purporting to explain a host of apparently unconnected events with only a few concepts, the sweeping formulation becomes a banner around which adherents and critics rally in wordy conflict. The proposition is often adopted, of course, because it is consistent with its supporters' own preconceptions. But similarly, many of the attacks stem from its challenge to alternative conceptual structures. Psychology can point to several such controversial formulations—for example, the Oedipus complex, Hull's contention that learning requires drive reduction, and the cognitive consistency notions. Although they differ in scope these crucial integrative propositions all represent important theoretical issues, and the controversies that swirl around them are often quite beneficial. Many of the investigations addressed

1

to these disputes touch on matters central to the science in general, and thus have far-reaching ramifications.

The frustration-aggression hypothesis is one of these crucial formulations. In one way or another, this hypothesis has stimulated or profoundly influenced hundreds of studies. More than this, however, much of the research bears upon issues that transcend the specific hypothesis: the question of innate determinants of human behavior, the traditional drive concept and the role of external stimuli versus endogenous motivation, the relationship between emotion and behavior, the operation of anticipation in motivated action, and, of course, the definition of frustration. The experimental literature dealing with these matters is extremely relevant to the frustration-aggression hypothesis, and similarly, frustration-aggression research, properly designed, can make important contributions to the general field of experimental psychology.

Before considering some of the issues just mentioned, it will be helpful to indicate my own position in this controversy. Basically, I believe a frustrating event increases the probability that the thwarted organism will act aggressively soon afterward, and that this relationship exists in many different animal species, including man. This acceptance of the central thesis of the frustration-aggression hypothesis does not mean complete agreement with the version formulated by Dollard, Doob, Miller, Mowrer, and Sears in their classic monograph, *Frustration and Aggression* (1939). Almost thirty years have gone by, and additional information has been acquired. There is now good reason to believe, as I will try to show in this chapter, that their major proposition is at once too simple and too sweeping. Contrary to their original argument, the existence of frustration *does not* always lead to some form of aggression, and the occurrence of aggressive behavior *does not necessarily* presuppose the existence of frustration. Aggression is a much more complicated phenomenon than the 1939 statement would have us think.

Because of these complications, we will not deal here with

instrumental aggression or the learning of aggressiveness habits. The analysis of aggression is difficult enough even if we confine ourselves to relatively brief time periods—from just before to just after the thwarting. Awareness of the problems in analyzing aggression, nevertheless, compels a modification rather than a complete rejection of the frustration-aggression hypothesis. Under some conditions, there *is* an increased likelihood of aggressive behavior following a frustration. In this discussion, aggression.will be defined as behavior whose goal response is the inflicting of injury on some object or person (cf. Berkowitz, 1962, 1965a). The behavior may be overt (physical or verbal) or may be implicit (in the case of thoughts). Aggression, then, is distinguished from an emotional state (anger or general arousal) which may facilitate and perhaps even "energize" the aggressive response.

INNATE RELATIONSHIP BETWEEN FRUSTRATION AND AGGRESSION

As I have noted in other papers (e.g., Berkowitz, 1965a), some attacks on the frustration-aggression hypothesis actually derive from objections to the notion of "built-in" sources of human behavior. Many writers apparently view the frustration-aggression hypothesis as implying an innate connection between an antecedent stimulus event, the frustration, and the subsequent aggressive response. Dollard and his colleagues seem to have thought in these terms when they wrote, "the frustration-aggression hypothesis assumes a universal causal relation between frustration and aggression" (1939, p. 10), although Neal Miller stated two years later that "no assumptions are made as to whether the frustration-aggression relationship is of innate or of learned origin" (Miller, 1941, p. 340). Be that as it may, the implication is there for many psychologists, and critics have argued against it. Bandura and Walters, in their influential book, *Social Learning and Personality Development*, point to the role of learning in modifying frustration reactions and cite this as evidence of the inadequacy of the frustration-aggression hypothesis (1963, pp. 135–137). Their position seems to be that the presence of learning, at least in humans, excludes the possibility of innate behavioral determinants. However, learning and innate determination can coexist in man (cf. Berkowitz, 1965a, p. 308). As Miller wrote some years ago in suggesting that there are built-in patterns of human behavior, these patterns may be modifiable enough so that they are disguised by learning but may still play a crucial role in motivating socially-learned behavior (Miller, 1964, p. 160). The frustration-aggression relationship may be *learnable* without being entirely *learned*.

Experiments with animals show that thwartings may lead to aggressive behavior even without prior learning. This is reported, for example, by Azrin, Hutchinson, and Hake (1966) in their study of pigeons (Chapter 3 in this volume). Socially isolated birds who were suddenly deprived of food rewards after a reinforcement period attacked another pigeon in the cage with them just as did nonisolated birds. "The attack behavior was not a result of a history of competition over food," the investigators concluded. Moving up the evolutionary ladder, Seay and Harlow (1965) found that six-month-old rhesus monkeys who were frustrated by being separated from their mothers exhibited aggression toward a peer even though aggression is extremely rare at this age and the infants probably had not learned to act aggressively prior to the separation. Also attesting to the unlearned basis of aggression, according to Hutchinson, Ulrich, and Azrin (1965), was the finding that electric shocks produced fighting in pairs of rats raised in isolation from the time of weaning, although not as much as in socially experienced rats. Ulrich has observed that "the fact that subjects with no history of social interaction did fight indicates that pain-elicited aggression has an instinctive, or unconditioned basis . . ." (Ulrich, 1966, p. 653).

I do not necessarily generalize from these animal studies to human behavior. Unlike those writers who have been all too quick to jump from fish to geese to man (e.g., Lorenz, 1966), most social scientists prefer to exhibit due caution in making these extrapolations. But caution does not mean rejection of all generalizations from animals to humans. Zajonc, a social psychologist, has suggested that "unless we have a good *a priori* reason to believe otherwise, it is best to act as if a generalization made about behavior applies universally to all species" (1966, p. 17). If we follow this lead, then, we would have to question those psychologists who *insist* that people have to learn to act aggressively in response to a frustration (e.g., Bandura and Walters, 1963; Kuhn, Madsen, and Becker, 1967).

DEFINITION OF FRUSTRATION

What is a frustration? Critics of the frustration-aggression hypothesis have rightly objected to the vagueness of the concept "frustration." This word is one of the many psychological terms originating in common speech which are susceptible to radically different definitions. It has been used in different ways by psychologists (cf. Britt and Janus, 1940), generally referring either to the external instigating condition or to the organism's reaction to this condition. A few examples readily illustrate the confusion surrounding the term. Dollard, Doob *et al.* (1939) confined their use of the concept to external events, and refused to make any inferences about internal emotional states with the exception of some hypothetical "instigation to aggression."[1] On the other hand, Brown and Farber (1951), Amsel (1958), and others thought of frustration as an internal reaction. However, although these latter writers agreed in employing the word as an intervening construct with emotional or motivational properties, they differed in their conception of the antecedents of this internal state. Indeed, most of the difficulties faced by the frustration-aggression hypothesis arise from uncertainties in the specification of these antecedent conditions.

Here again, consider the disagreement and confusion. In

their classic formulation, the Yale psychologists defined frustration as "an interference with the occurrence of an instigated goal-response at its proper time in the behavior sequence" (Dollard *et al.*, 1939, p. 7). This statement, it seems to me, could be modified somewhat. It should note explicitly that goal responses must be in operation, whether implicitly or overtly, and prevented from achieving consummation if there is to be a resulting instigation to aggression. Because of this ambiguity, some writers have equated frustration with the omission of a customary reward, i.e., a deprivation, whether or not the organism was engaged in consummatory or even instrumental activity relative to that reward. This failure to distinguish between deprivation and frustration can account for some of the negative results in tests of the frustration-aggression hypothesis, and it is also involved in the emphasis upon "arbitrary" frustrations as the sole source of aggressive reactions to thwartings (Pastore, 1952; Cohen, 1955). As I have suggested elsewhere (1962, pp. 66–67), the individual facing a "nonarbitrary" barrier to his goal, or who expects such an interference, may actually cease his goal-directed activity. ("If it is proper that I not reach my goal now, I won't try to get to it now.") Goal-oriented behavior slackens and anticipatory goal responses weaken. Thus, the reasonable and/or expected obstacle may not be a real frustration; there may not be any instigated goal responses on that occasion.[2]

Many different operations have been employed as frustrations, whether the conceptual meaning is interference with the attainment of a customary reward or prevention of the consummation of instigated goal responses. Reflecting this diversity of approaches, Buss (1961, pp. 17–20) suggested that the blocking of any action typically leading to a reinforcer could be regarded as a frustration. The blocking could stem from external barriers to the completion of a chain of instrumental responses, failure to obtain a reward, omission of the reward, internal conflict between incompatible responses, or prevention of the individual's appropriate consummatory response. As previously noted, even those theorists who define frustrations as internal reactions are not entirely agreed on the antecedent conditions. Amsel's (1958, 1962) important conception singled out nonreward as the frustration-inducing operation, while Brown and Farber (1951) saw internal conflict as the essential origin of the emotional response. The conflict could be produced, they hypothesized, by interference with an ongoing behavior sequence arising from either inhibitions or a competing motivated action tendency.

Clearly, research into the relation between frustration and aggression requires greater consensus as to the theoretical meaning of "frustration" and the operations that could be employed in establishing the theoretically relevant antecedent conditions. Many of the failures to confirm the frustration-aggression hypothesis reflect the vagueness of the terms in the hypothesis—particularly frustration—rather than the formulation's essential lack of validity. This last point cannot be stressed too much, I believe. A good deal of psychological research is still directed toward tests of the frustration-aggression hypothesis despite considerable evidence demonstrating that frustrations *can* heighten the probability of aggressive behavior. Rather than merely testing the notion again and again, we should address ourselves to the inconsistent findings. Under what conditions does a thwarting lead to an aggressive reaction? Part of the answer to this question demands a more precise definition of frustration.

EVIDENCE FOR THE FRUSTRATION-AGGRESSION RELATIONSHIP

Only a few studies need be cited in order to show that frustrations can cause aggression. Important evidence is provided, for example, by Azrin, Hutchinson, and Hake (1966) in Chapter 3, as mentioned earlier. Pigeons were taught to peck at a key by reinforcing them with food every time they carried out the action. Then, after the key-pressing response was well established, the investigators suddenly stopped giving the birds food for their behavior. If another pigeon was in the cage at this time—and I shall return to this point later—the thwarted animals would attack it, even to the extent of pulling out feathers from the target bird. Other observations indicated, moreover, that the aggression was not simply a displacement of the conditioned key-pecking responses; extinction-induced aggression was also displayed by pigeons who previously were given food automatically and had not been required to peck at a key in order to obtain the reward.

Research with young children also testifies to the aggressive consequences of at least some frustrations. In one study (Elbert and Ulrich, cited in Ulrich, 1966, p. 660), ten-year-old youngsters given the task of stacking bottle stoppers in order to earn money exhibited sharp increases in aggression toward a peer after this person had supposedly interfered with their work by shaking their table. Of course, the frustration treatment used in this experiment might conceivably have been interpreted by the subjects as a deliberate attack on them. The younger children in the Mallick and McCandless (1966) study could also have viewed their thwarting in this manner. In this experiment (Chapter 6 in this volume) eight- and nine-year-old boys and girls had to perform a simple construction task in order to earn money. Even though their peer's "inadvertently clumsy" behavior prevented some of the subjects from completing their assignment, the frustrater coupled his interference with sarcastic remarks. Various aggression measures were obtained in the three investigations carried out by the researchers: number of electric shocks administered to the peer, number of presses on a button that supposedly would interfere with the peer's work, and questionnaire ratings of like or dislike for him. For each of these measures, the frustrated subjects exhibited stronger aggression than did the nonfrustrated controls.

Other studies included in this book employed adult humans as subjects. In the experiment by Buss (1963)—Chapter 4—

men and women college students found that they were unable
to teach a concept to a partner (by punishing him for mistakes),
and therefore could not gain a reward—either the approbation
of the experimenter, or a higher course grade, or money. These
subjects subsequently displayed stronger attacks on the frustrating slow learner than did other subjects who did not have
an incentive for rapid teaching and who expected their partner
to take a long time to learn the concept. Frustration led to intensified aggression, Buss concluded, even though the thwarting was nonarbitrary and the aggression was not instrumental
to the attainment of other goals. He also observed, however,
that the level of aggression shown by the frustrated subjects
was not very great relative to the level possible in the situation.

The experiment reported by Geen and Berkowitz (1967),
Chapter 7 in this volume, suggests that inhibitions against aggression can sometimes mask the aggressive reaction to a
thwarting. The male college students in this investigation were
first given one of three arousal treatments. Each was asked to
complete a jigsaw puzzle, supposedly as a test of his ability to
form spatial patterns. In one-third of the cases, the subjects were
unable to finish the task because the puzzle actually was insoluble. Another third of the men were insulted by a confederate
after they had failed on the puzzle, while the remaining subjects were neither frustrated nor insulted. After this, each person witnessed either a violent prize fight movie or a film of an
exciting but nonviolent track race. Equally important, the prize
fight scene was given an introduction that lowers inhibitions
against aggression (Berkowitz and Rawlings, 1963; Berkowitz,
1965b; Berkowitz and Geen, 1967). As soon as the film was
over, the subject had a socially sanctioned opportunity to shock
the person he had encountered earlier (i.e., the confederate),
employing the Buss procedure. Of those who had seen the track
film, only the men deliberately insulted by their peer gave significantly more intense shocks to him than did the nonaroused
control subjects. For the subjects shown the fight film, however,
both the insulted *and* task-frustrated men exhibited stronger

attacks on the confederate than did the nonaroused subjects. The aggressive movie had apparently lowered restraints against frustration-engendered aggression.

A later experiment by Geen (1967) clarifies a possible source of doubt in the above Geen-Berkowitz study. Since the task-frustrated men in the earlier experiment had seen the confederate finish the jigsaw puzzle while they had not been able to do the job, these subjects might have regarded the failure as a blow to their self-esteem. Three groups of subjects in the Geen experiment also were unable to complete the assigned jigsaw puzzle. In one group, the subjects worked alone without knowledge of how the others had performed. In another group, the subjects were distracted by the bumbling interference of a confederate who later acknowledged that he had been responsible for the subjects' inability to do the puzzle. And in the last group, each subject was insulted by the confederate after the subject failed in the task. Following this, all subjects saw the prize fight film with the inhibition-reducing "justified aggression" introduction. All three groups subsequently administered stronger shocks to the confederate in the Buss procedure than did those in a nonaroused control condition.

Inhibitions can also contribute to the low level of overt aggression resulting from a "nonarbitrary" frustration. Basing their arguments primarily on subjects' descriptions of what they would do in hypothetical situations (cf. Pastore, 1952; Cohen, 1955), a number of writers have contended that people do not become aggressive following some thwarting if they believe the interference to their goal attainment was justified by acceptable rules; only arbitrary frustrations supposedly led to aggression. There is no good evidence for this position, however. As Pastore (1952, p. 730) acknowledged, we may not care to reveal our aggressive reactions when a socially proper frustration has been inflicted on us. The Burnstein and Worchel (1962) experiment described in Chapter 5 supports this possibility. Groups of male undergraduates were prevented from reaching their goal, a unanimous decision on an assigned problem, because of a fellow group member's persistent questions and interruptions. In the nonarbitrary frustration condition, this task interference was readily attributable to the questioner's obvious hearing defect, but no such justifiable explanation was present in the arbitrary frustration condition. When the group members were later asked whether they wanted to exclude anyone from their group, public rejection of the interfering member occurred only in the arbitrary frustration condition and not in the nonarbitrary frustration groups. Nevertheless, other findings showed that the frustrating group member was also rejected by some subjects, even when he had justification for his interference with the group's progress, in more private expressions of opinion. The subjects had evidently inhibited the public display of hostility toward their frustrater when his interference was nonarbitrary. There were also signs of displaced hostility in the nonarbitrary frustration condition. The men in these groups rated both themselves and the experimenter less favorably than did the subjects experiencing the arbitrary frustration, presumably because the former had refrained from showing their aggression toward the hard-of-hearing group member who had had a "legitimate" excuse for frustrating them.

Thus, contrary to arguments raised by writers such as Maslow (1941), frustrations *can* produce aggressive reactions, even when the thwarting does not represent a threat to the personality. This relationship between frustration and aggression, furthermore, seems to hold in a wide variety of animal species.

NONAGGRESSIVE FRUSTRATION REACTIONS AND NONFRUSTRATIVE AGGRESSION

To say that frustrations can heighten the probability of aggressive behavior does not necessarily mean every thwarting will lead inevitably to an attack upon any available (and safe) target in the situation. Even if inhibitions against aggression are weak, overt aggression may not occur on a given occasion if (a) the individual has learned to make a nonaggressive reaction in that type of situation, and/or (b) the available target does not have appropriate stimulus qualities.

Neal Miller's (1941) paper—Chapter 2 of this volume—is addressed to the first of these contingencies. Two years after the publication of the original monograph, Miller discussed the two-part generalization his colleagues and he had offered. The first half of the original proposition was defensible, he contended: "The occurrence of aggression always presupposes the existence of frustration." He did want the second part modified, however. Instead of saying that "the existence of frustration always leads to some form of aggression," he now preferred a less "unclear and misleading" proposition: "Frustration produces instigations to a number of different types of response, one of which is an instigation to some form of aggression." Some people may have acquired the habit of responding nonaggressively to frustrations, and these nonaggressive reactions could inhibit aggression. Nevertheless, if the first responses did not reduce the strength of the thwarted instigation, these alternative, nonaggressive reactions would weaken so that the next strongest response tendencies would occur. Aggression eventually would be displayed if the instigation to the blocked responses persisted.

An experiment by Otis and McCandless (1955) with nursery school children illustrates the role of both individual differences in frustration reactions and persistent thwartings. When the youngsters were individually prevented from moving a toy over an assigned path, those who had earlier been rated as having strong power-dominance needs showed a greater increase in aggressive behavior over the eight frustration trials than did the others. Aggression evidently ranked higher in the hierarchy of responses to frustration for the high-dominance preschoolers than for the low-dominance children. As the blocking continued over the eight trials, frustration reactions inconsistent with aggression dropped out more rapidly in the high-dominance youngsters than in the children with weak power-dominance needs; the high-dominance subjects exhibited a greater increase in aggression than did the low-dominance children from the first four to the last four trials. But even the youngsters rated as having strong needs for love and affection began to act somewhat more aggressively in the later trials, and their non-aggressive frustration reactions also tended to weaken.

In spite of this supporting evidence, we must modify Miller's analysis of continued frustrations. Persistent frustrations may not always lead to strong aggressive reactions. The present analysis maintains that aggression will result only when antici-patory goal responses are in operation and the blocking prevents goal responses from achieving consummation—that is, when the person has anticipated reaching a goal but is blocked from doing so. Obviously, if he expected his efforts to be thwarted, he would not anticipate getting to the goal, and his goal striving might weaken or disappear altogether (cf. Berkowitz, 1960; Berkowitz, 1962, pp. 64–66, for further discussion). People ex-periencing continued frustrations often become generally apa-thetic. They give up trying. Omission of rewards is then a deprivation rather than a frustration for them.

We should also introduce another qualification of the original formulation at this time. Where the Yale psychologists had maintained that all aggression presupposes a frustration—a defensible proposition, according to Miller (1941)—more re-cent research questions this supposition. Animals at times act aggressively even when there is no reason to think they are frustrated (Lagerspetz and Nurmi, 1964; Moyer, 1967; Scott, 1966). People may learn to aggress much as they learn to display any other type of behavior (cf. Bandura and Walters, 1963). This has been demonstrated especially well in experi-ments on modeling influences. In the important studies by Bandura, Ross, and Ross, for example, nursery school children exposed to an aggressive adult model tended to imitate the adult's behavior (1961). This type of influence manifested itself whether the adult was with the children during the observation situation, was on film, or was dressed as a nonrealistic cartoon character (1963a). Imitative aggression was particularly likely to occur when the model was seen being rewarded for aggression rather than being punished (1963b). The observation of aggression can have a relatively long-lasting effect, moreover. According to other research (Hicks, 1965), nursery school children may imitate an adult male's aggressive actions six months after viewing his violent behavior.

Of course, these observational effects are influenced by the person's prior experiences. Young boys and girls do not react in the same way to witnessed violence (Bandura, Ross, and Ross, 1963b; Hicks, 1965). A history of frequent frustrations, as well as prior reinforcement for aggressive actions, might perhaps determine whether the observed violence leads to aggressive consequences. While immediately experienced frustrations can increase the likelihood that witnessed aggression produces strong aggressive reactions, as Geen and Berkowitz report in Chapter 7, recent thwartings may not be necessary for modeling influences to occur.

AVERSIVE EVENTS AND ANTICIPATORY GOAL RESPONSES

The frustration-aggression relationship can be more readily accepted if we do not think of the frustration reaction as affectively neutral. Amsel (1962), Azrin *et al.* (1966), Ulrich (1966), and others have noted that frustrative nonreward has many of the properties of punishment. According to an experiment by Ferster (1957), for example, the withdrawal of a positive conditioned reinforcer serves as a punishment for pigeons.

Organisms evidently find frustrative nonreward aversive, much as pain-producing shocks are aversive stimuli—and pain is a very reliable cause of aggression (cf. Ulrich, 1966). This conception of frustration as an aversive state has an immediate implication for my 1962 discussion of the frustration-aggression hypothesis. Following McDougall, I had suggested that at least some painful events might be frustrating in the sense that they interfered with certain forms of want satisfaction (1962, p. 30). If we adopt the Amsel view, however, we can reverse the analogy and conceive of frustrations as aversive events similar to pain-producing or at least unpleasant situations.

But as I proposed earlier in this chapter, an adequately detailed version of the frustration-aggression hypothesis should consider the anticipatory goal responses (or expectations) that are prevented from reaching fulfillment. Of course, theorists as different as Spence (1956) and Atkinson (1964) generally think of all motivated behavior as involving the operation of anticipatory goal responses or expectations, so all we might want to say in many cases is that there was interference with ongoing, motivated behavior. Specific reference to the nonconsummation of anticipatory goal responses, however, can help determine when a nonreward is a *frustrative* nonreward; the frustrated organism, to put it simply, was anticipating a reward which did not materialize or was not satisfactorily consummated. As one of the authors of the 1939 *Frustration and Aggression* observed some years later, frustration exists primarily "when there is appetitive involvement, and what may be called the *intent* to gratify the primary drive" (Mowrer, 1949, cited in Yates, 1962, p. 110). To use another term favored by Mowrer, there is a frustration when a hope is dashed.

The politico-social counterpart of this formulation is obvious; the phrase "revolution of rising expectations" refers to just this conception of frustration. Poverty-stricken groups who have never dreamed of having automobiles, washing machines, or new homes are not frustrated because they have been deprived of these things; they are frustrated only after they have begun to hope. If they dare to think they might get these objects and anticipate their satisfactions, the inability to fulfill their anticipations is a frustration. Privations in themselves are much less likely to breed violence than is the dashing of hopes.

James Davies (1962) has employed this type of reasoning in his theory of revolutions (Chapter 8 in this volume). The American, French, and Russian Revolutions did not arise because these people were subjected to prolonged, severe hardships, Davies suggested. In each of these revolutions, and others as well, the established order was overthrown when a sudden, sharp socioeconomic decline abruptly thwarted the hopes and expectations that had begun to develop in the course of gradually improving conditions. Some data recently reported by Feierabend and Feierabend (1966) can also be understood in these terms. They applied the frustration-aggression hypothesis to the study of political instability in a very impressive cross-national investigation. They observed, among other findings, that rapid change in modernization within a society (as indicated by such measurements as the percentage of persons having a primary education and the per capita consumption of calories) was associated with a relatively great increase in political instability (p. 265). It could be that rapid socioeconomic improvements produce more hopes and expectations than can be fulfilled. Hope outstrips reality, even though conditions are rapidly improving for the society as a whole, and many of the people in the society are frustrated.

Other observations are also consistent with this emphasis on the nonconsummation of anticipatory goal responses. In Chapter 3, Azrin and his co-workers (1966) report, for example, that their pigeons attacked the target bird mainly when the extinction followed the actual eating of food. "No attack resulted if the pigeon was prevented from eating either by a physical obstruction or by prior satiation. The mere sight of food did not produce appreciable attack." It could be that the sight of food had not elicited goal responses in sufficient strength so that the subsequent nonconsummation of food yielded only a mild reaction. Similarly, the thwarted birds' duration of attack against a stuffed target pigeon was a direct function of the number of food deliveries preceding extinction—a factor which would heighten anticipatory eating responses before the onset of the frustrative nonreward.

Berkowitz (1966) has also reported that the nonfulfillment of expectations can increase aggressive responses. In this experiment, half of the angered men were led to believe they would soon have an opportunity to attack their tormentor, while the remainder of the provoked subjects were informed that they would not be able to attack this person right away. Then, supposedly because the experimenter had made a mistake, half of the men found that their anticipations were not confirmed: they could not aggress after expecting to be able to, or could attack their frustrater after not expecting to have this aggressive opportunity. The expectations created by the experimenter's prior instructions were fulfilled for the other half of the men so that some of these aggressed as they had expected to be able to do. Shortly after, all subjects were given a socially sanctioned opportunity to aggress against the anger instigator. Two separate aggression measures—number of electric shocks and an adjective checklist—showed that the strongest attacks were made by men whose previous aggressive anticipations had *not* been fulfilled. The information about their forthcoming aggressive opportunity had evidently evoked anticipatory aggressive responses in these subjects. The subsequent inability to consummate these responses by attacking the person they had been set to injure was frustrating, and this led to the stronger aggression against this person.

AGGRESSION-ELICITING STIMULI AND POSTFRUSTRATION REACTIONS

Several of my recent papers have argued for the role of aggression-eliciting stimuli in impulsive aggression (e.g., Berkowitz, 1964, 1965a; Berkowitz and Green, 1962; Berkowitz and

Buck, 1967). The position taken was a simple one: Frustration-produced emotion arousal theoretically created only a readiness for aggressive behavior; aggressive cues—stimuli associated with aggression or with the frustraters—presumably were necessary if aggressive responses were actually to occur. Thus, the impulsive attack following a frustrating experience was supposedly "pulled out" by appropriate cues in the situation rather than "pushed out" by strong emotional excitation. The target was attacked impulsively because he had evoked strong aggressive responses from the aroused person. Somewhat reminiscent of Buss' (1961) doubts about the notion of anger as *the* aggressive drive, this reasoning suggested that the frustration-engendered emotion only (a) somehow facilitated the occurrence of an aggressive reaction to the aggressive cues—this phenomenon is often described as "energizing" the reaction—and (b) decreased possible aggression-inhibiting responsivity to peripheral stimuli in the situation.

In this chapter I will backtrack somewhat from this extreme position. Instead of saying that these externally derived aggressive cues are necessary for aggression to occur, my thesis will be: The emotional state arising from the encounter with the aversive stimulus may in itself contain distinctive stimuli which can instigate the aggressive reaction, particularly if the emotion is strong enough; but the presence of appropriate aggressive cues (in the external environment or represented internally in thoughts) increases the probability that an overt aggressive response will actually take place.

As I suggested in an earlier discussion of the 1939 frustration-aggression hypothesis (Berkowitz, 1962, pp. 107–108), Dollard and his colleagues implicitly recognized the importance of the available target's stimulus properties. This can be seen in the proposition that "the agent perceived to be the source of the frustration" is most likely to be attacked by the thwarted individual (Dollard *et al.,* 1939, p. 39), and also in Miller's (1948) translation of the psychoanalytic concept of hostility displacement into stimulus-response generalization terms. The target person is attacked, these statements suggest, because of his stimulus qualities, and these qualities presumably derive, at least in part, from association with the aversive event.

A variety of animal experiments demonstrates that an object's possession of certain stimulus properties increases the likelihood that it will be attacked following some arousal manipulation. Adding to the observations I have cited elsewhere (Berkowitz, 1965a), Azrin and his colleagues report in Chapter 3 that only 25 per cent of the thwarted pigeons attacked a stuffed target pigeon, whereas all pigeons attacked a live target bird. Some of this difference is probably attributable to the target object's movement (even if only movement of the head). A moving object is more distinctive than a stationary one, and any distinctive stimulus might perhaps be attacked. But for some animals at least, more than movement per se is necessary to elicit an attack. Lagerspetz and Mettala (1965) administered painful electric shocks to the feet of laboratory mice. These animals exhibited aggressive responses toward a bottle brush presented as a possible target only when the brush was moved, but the aggression was more intense when the brush was rotated rather than moved in a pendular fashion. Sometimes the qualitative characteristics of the available target combine with the target's movements in determining the magnitude of the aggressive response. In their study with electrically shocked rats, Ulrich and Azrin (1962) found that the aroused animals did not attack a doll, whether this object was still or moved rapidly about the cage. A recently deceased rat, by contrast, was attacked when it was moved about the cage on a stick, but not when it was stationary. "A second moving animal," they concluded, "is a necessary condition for eliciting the fighting response from a rat stimulated by foot-shock."

Essentially similar observations have been reported in experiments dealing with aggression produced by hypothalamic stimulation. As only one example, Levison and Flynn (1965) found that stimulated cats were relatively unlikely to attack blocks of styrofoam or foam rubber. The probability of persistent aggression rose as the investigators changed the available target from a stuffed rat to an anesthetized rat and, finally, to an unanesthetized rat. Whether the aggressive predisposition was created by stimulation of the hypothalamus or electric shocks to the foot, the presence of objects having particular stimulus qualities evidently increased the likelihood that this predisposition would lead to aggressive behavior. We are dealing here with a widespread phenomenon. Upon surveying animal research literature, Moyer has recently concluded: "Aggression is generally stimulus bound." For many types of aggression, he has noted, "the stimulus situation to which the S will react with hostility is highly specific" (1967, p. 4).

Much additional experimentation is required, obviously, before we can specify just what stimulus properties are capable of eliciting aggression and what processes underlie the origin and operation of this effect. These investigations undoubtedly will be confronted by a number of highly complex issues. Thus, the aggression-eliciting stimuli probably vary from species to species, and even from one type of aggression to another. In regard to this last complication, Moyer (1967) has insisted that an adequate understanding of aggresion-evoking stimuli requires differentiation among types of aggression. His list covers *irritable aggression* (resulting from frustration, and increases in drive and pain), *predatory aggression, intermale spontaneous aggression, terror-induced aggression, territorial defense, defense of the young,* and *instrumental aggression.* Other writers (e.g., Roberts and Kiess, 1964) have distinguished between predatory attack and affective aggression, pointing out that the animal's behavior is not the same in the two cases. Whatever classes of aggression are established, the stimuli evoking them probably differ in important respects.

As I also indicated earlier, some aggressive acts following aversive stimulation may not be evoked by external stimuli. Ulrich reported, for example, that hooded rats fought much less frequently after being shocked than did other, nonhooded animals—but pain-elicited aggression still occurred (1966, p.

651). Similarly, in his recent review of research on the agonistic behavior of mice and rats, Scott (1966, p. 689) observed that blinded mice do fight; visual signals were not absolutely necessary. The pain in and of itself might evoke fighting responses. All in all, the most parsimonious statement we might make about the role of external aggression-eliciting stimuli is this: The external stimulus somehow facilitates the occurrence of aggression but (somewhat in opposition to my earlier strong position) may not be necessary for aggression to take place.

Several reasons may be advanced for this increased probability of aggression in the presence of particular stimuli.

1. In some instances, the internal arousal state created by the aversive condition might function as a general drive capable of "energizing" many different forms of behavior. The external aggressive cue could then serve as either a conditioned or an unconditioned stimulus eliciting the associated aggressive responses. The external stimulus here was necessary for *aggression* to take place.

2. If the stimulus only *facilitates* the occurrence of aggression, however, taking off from Spence (1956), we might think of the external stimulus as evoking anticipatory aggressive responses, either because of prior conditioning, early imprinting, or possibly even some built-in reactivity to particular forms of external stimuli. The internal stimuli arising from these anticipatory aggressive responses might add to the already existing aggressive stimuli, and perhaps even to the general arousal state produced within the organism by the aversive event. Because of this aggressive increment, the aggressive responses are more likely to cross the threshold and appear in overt action.

3. Another intriguing possibility has recently been proposed by Glickman and Schiff (1967). Their theory contends that the facilitation of activity in the neural systems mediating species-specific consummatory acts is a sufficient condition for reinforcement. An external stimulus would be reinforcing to the extent that it facilitated neural activity in the operating motor paths. If implicit aggressive responses were already in

operation, an external stimulus "smoothing" the activity in the neural systems mediating the performance of aggressive goal responses presumably would be reinforcing. Findings obtained by Azrin, Hutchinson, and McLaughlin (1965) can be understood in this manner. Squirrel monkeys given painful electric shocks pulled a chain lowering a ball which could be attacked. Little or no chain-pulling occurred and very few attacks on the ball took place if the animals were not shocked. The ball evidently was a reinforcing stimulus. The sight of this available target could have smoothed the ongoing neural activity involved in the performance of the aggressive responses elicited by the shocks. Similarly, for other animals, the presence of an object having certain stimulus qualities could facilitate the neural activity involved in the aggressive responses evoked by aversive events, and thereby increase the probability that these responses would become overt.

ASSOCIATION WITH AGGRESSION OR FRUSTRATION SOURCE

Whatever the mechanisms producing the effect, stimuli associated with aggression generally or with the source of the present or previous thwartings presumably can evoke aggressive responses (Berkowitz, 1962, 1964, 1965a). Thus, as one obvious illustration, provoked subjects administered stronger attacks upon their tormentor when a rifle and pistol were nearby than when either a neutral object or no relevant object was present (Berkowitz and LePage, 1967). The weapons, as aggressive stimuli, elicited strong aggressive responses from the aroused men. Mallick and McCandless (1966) observed a similar effect in their investigations (Chapter 6). The non-provoked children given toy guns to play with subsequently were more aggressive toward the confederate than were the other nonaroused youngsters. Aggression-eliciting stimuli can also govern the consequences of observed violence. An anger instigator was attacked more intensely following an aggressive movie if his name connected him with the witnessed aggression than if he was not associated with the violent scene (cf. Berkowitz, 1965a, b). The name-mediated connection with the aggressive movie apparently enhanced the available target's cue value for aggression.

Geen and the author (1967) made use of this last-mentioned phenomenon in the investigation of the frustration-aggression relationship included in this book (Chapter 7). As shown, emotionally aroused male college students exhibited stronger aggression toward a peer after witnessing a boxing movie when the target-person's name associated him with the victim of the filmed violence than when he did not have the same name as the movie victim. This happened, furthermore, whether the arousal treatment was a direct insult or a task frustration. Indeed, if the available target did not have the name-mediated connection with the aggressive movie, only the insulted group displayed reliably stronger attacks than the nonaroused control group. When the name-mediated association existed, on the other hand, and the target's cue value for aggression was therefore high, both the frustrated and insulted men made significantly stronger attacks than their controls. An appropriate stimulus object had to be present in this study in order to have a clear demonstration of the possible aggressive consequences of a frustration.

Two recent (and unpublished) experiments by Knurek and myself also document the role of aggressive cues in frustration reactions. Where the target-person in the preceding Geen-Berkowitz investigation had also aroused the subjects, he was an "innocent bystander" in the more recent studies. In the first of these, men who could not win a money prize because of their partners' mistakes subsequently attributed more unfavorable characteristics to another person bearing the same name as their frustrater than to a third individual having a neutral name. Similarly, in the second experiment, subjects administered reliably more shocks to an innocent target-person after having been insulted by someone else (in comparison to the number given by nonaroused controls) only when the bystander had the same name as the insulter. The innocent individual's name-mediated association with the prior aversive agent caused him to elicit strong aggression from the aroused men, whether the aggression was on an adjective checklist or in the form of electric shocks.[3]

The present analysis also suggests a possible method for reducing the occurrence of aggressive behavior. If aggressive stimuli in the external environment increase the probability that frustrated people will attack someone, the likelihood of aggression should be lessened (but not eliminated altogether) if aggressive cues are removed from the situation. One way to do this is to alter the stimulus properties of the available target. Let us assume, for example, that a person seen as intending to aggress possesses a strong cue value for aggression (cf. Epstein and Taylor, 1967). The frustrater's chance of being attacked might be lessened—but not wiped out entirely—if he is labeled as *not* having wanted to hurt, i.e., if he is less of an *aggressive* stimulus. The Mallick and McCandless paper included in this volume (Chapter 6) contains some relevant data. In this study, thwarted youngsters who were informed that their frustrater had not meant to spoil their game subsequently exhibited less aggression toward him than did any of the other frustrated children.

Of course, we can explain this last finding in at least two ways: the frustrater's cue value for aggression could have been weakened, or the subjects could have inhibited their attacks upon him because they then viewed his interference as a "nonarbitrary frustration." Aggression supposedly was not justified. (In either case, we need not say there was a "catharsis" of aggression, the term used by the investigators.) For that matter, this change in the frustrater's stimulus qualities could also be involved in nonarbitrary thwartings. Defining a frustration as reasonable or proper, i.e., as nonarbitrary, in essence weakens the frustrater's association with aggression; his aggressive cue value is diminished. As a consequence, he would be less likely to elicit overt aggression from the frustrated individual. Further research is obviously necessary here as in the other aspects of aggression.

NOTES

The author's research summarized here was supported by grants from the National Science Foundation.

1. As I have noted elsewhere (1962, p. 32), Mowrer, one of the original authors of the 1939 monograph, later questioned the omission of "the intervening variable of anger" from the "simple stimulus-response framework" guiding the initial formulation (Mowrer, 1960, pp. 404–405).

2. There are two other possibilities. First, and most obvious, people may also inhibit their aggressive reactions if they believe aggressive behavior is unwarranted because of the reasonable nature of the thwarting (Berkowitz, 1962, pp. 40–41; Rothaus and Worchel, 1960). Presumably because of these inhibitions against aggression, Burnstein and Worchel (1962) obtained indications of greater hostility displacement by subjects confronted by a nonarbitrary frustration than by people experiencing an arbitrary thwarting. Second, as I will suggest at the end of this chapter, interpreting the frustrater as not having had an aggressive intent might conceivably lessen his ability to evoke aggressive responses even in the absence of inhibitions.

3. Moore (1964) has also reported that aggression can generalize from a frustrater to a target having similar stimulus characteristics. In her experiment, frustrated boys expressed a greater desire to shoot at a card figure resembling the figure who had beaten them in a game than at a target-figure not having this resemblance to the frustrater.

REFERENCES

Amsel, A. The role of frustrative nonreward in noncontinuous reward situations. 55, *Psychological Bulletin*, 1958, 102–119.

Amsel, A. Frustrative nonreward in partial reinforcement and discrimination learning: Some recent history and a theoretical extension. 69, *Psychological Review*, 1962, 306–328.

Atkinson, J. W. *An Introduction to Motivation*. Princeton, N.J.: Van Nostrand, 1964.

Azrin, N. H., R. R. Hutchinson, and D. F. Hakel. Extinction-induced aggression. 9, *Journal of the Experimental Analysis of Behavior,* 1966, 191–204.

Azrin, N. H., R. R. Hutchinson, and R. McLaughlin. The opportunity for aggression as an operant reinforcer during aversive stimulation. 8, *Journal of the Experimental Analysis of Behavior,* 1965, 171–180.

Bandura, A., and R. H. Walters. *Social Learning and Personality Development.* New York: Holt, Rinehart & Winston, 1963.

Bandura, A., Dorothea Ross, and Sheila Ross. Transmission of aggression through imitation of aggressive models. 63, *Journal of Abnormal and Social Psychology,* 1961, 575–582.

Bandura, A., Dorothea Ross, and Sheila Ross. Imitation of film-mediated aggressive models. 66, *Journal of Abnormal and Social Psychology,* 1963a, 3–11.

Bandura, A., Dorothea Ross, and Sheila Ross. Vicarious reinforcement and imitative learning. 67, *Journal of Abnormal and Social Psychology,* 1963b, 601–607.

Berkowitz, L. Repeated frustrations and expectations in hostility arousal. 60, *Journal of Abnormal and Social Psychology,* 1960, 422–429.

Berkowitz, L. *Aggression: A Social Psychological Analysis.* New York: McGraw-Hill, 1962.

Berkowitz, L. Aggressive cues in aggressive behavior and hostility catharsis. 71, *Psychological Review,* 1964, 104–122.

Berkowitz, L. The concept of aggressive drive: Some additional considerations. In L. Berkowitz (ed.), *Advances in Experimental Social Psychology,* Vol. 2. New York: Academic Press, 1965a.

Berkowitz, L. Some aspects of observed aggression. 2, *Journal of Personality and Social Psychology,* 1965b, 359–369.

Berkowitz, L. On not being able to aggress. 5, *British Journal of Social and Clinical Psychology,* 1966, 130–139.

Berkowitz, L., and R. W. Buck. Impulsive aggression: Reactivity to aggressive cues under emotion arousal. 35, *Journal of Personality,* 1967, 415–424.

Berkowitz, L., and R. G. Geen. Stimulus qualities of the target of aggression: A further study. 5, *Journal of Personality and Social Psychology,* 1967, 364–368.

Berkowitz, L., and J. A. Green. The stimulus qualities of the scapegoat. 64, *Journal of Abnormal and Social Psychology,* 1962, 293–301.

Berkowitz, L., and A. LePage. Weapons as aggression-eliciting stimuli. 7, *Journal of Personality and Social Psychology,* 1967, 202–207.

Berkowitz, L., and Edna Rawlings. Effects of film violence on inhibitions against subsequent aggression. 66, *Journal of Abnormal and Social Psychology,* 1963, 405–412.

Britt, S. H., and S. Q. Janus. Criteria of frustration. 47, *Psychological Review,* 1940, 451–470.

Brown, J. S., and I. E. Farber. Emotions conceptualized as intervening variables—with suggestions toward a theory of frustration. 48, *Psychological Bulletin,* 1951, 465–495.

Burnstein, E., and P. Worchel. Arbitrariness of frustration and its consequences for aggression in a social situation. 30, *Journal of Personality,* 1962, 528–541.

Buss, A. H. *The Psychology of Aggression.* New York: Wiley, 1961.

Buss, A. H. Physical aggression in relation to different frustrations. 67, *Journal of Abnormal and Social Psychology*, 1963, 1–7.

Cohen, A. R. Social norms, arbitrariness of frustration, and status of the agent of frustration in the frustration-aggression hypothesis. 5, *Journal of Abnormal and Social Psychology*, 1955, 222–226.

Davies, J. C. Toward a theory of revolution, 27, *American Sociological Review*, 1962, 5–19.

Dollard, J., L. Doob, N. Miller, O. Mowrer, and R. Sears. *Frustration and Aggression*. New Haven: Yale University Press, 1939.

Epstein, S., and S. P. Taylor. Instigation to aggression as a function of degree of defeat and perceived aggressive intent of the opponent. 35, *Journal of Personality*, 1967, 265–289.

Feierabend, I. K., and Rosalind L. Feierabend. Aggression behaviors within politics, 1948-1962: A cross-national study. 10, *Journal of Conflict Resolution*, 1966, 249–271.

Ferster, C. B. Withdrawal of positive reinforcement as punishment. 126, *Science,* 1957, 509.

Geen, R. G. Frustration, attack, and prior training in aggressiveness as antecedents of aggressive behavior. Unpublished doctoral dissertation. University of Wisconsin, 1967.

Geen, R. G., and L. Berkowitz. Some conditions facilitating the occurrence of aggression after the observation of violence. *Journal of Personality,* 1967, 35, 666–676.

Glickman, S. E., and B. B. Schiff. A biological theory of reinforcement. 74, *Psychological Review,* 1967, 81–109.

Hicks, D. J. Imitation and retention of film-mediated aggressive peer and adult models. 2, *Journal of Personality and Social Psychology,* 1965, 97–100.

Hutchinson, R. R., R. E. Ulrich, and N. H. Azrin. Effects of age and related factors on the pain-aggression reaction. 59, *Journal of Comparative and Physiological Psychology,* 1965, 365–369.

Kuhn, Deanna Z., C. H. Madsen, Jr., and W. C. Becker. Effects of exposure to an aggressive model and frustration on children's aggressive behavior. 38, *Child Development,* 1967, 739–746.

Lagerspetz, Kirsti, and Raija Mettala. Stimulation experiments on stimuli eliciting aggressive behaviour in mice. *Report of the Psychological Institute, University of Turku, Finland,* 1965, No. 13.

Lagerspetz, Kirsti, and R. Nurmi. An experiment on the frustration-aggression hypothesis. *Report of the Psychological Institute, University of Turku, Finland,* 1964, No. 10.

Levison, P. K., and J. P. Flynn. The objects attacked by cats during stimulation of the hypothalamus. 13, *Animal Behaviour,* 1965, 217–220.

Levy, D. M. The hostile act. 48, *Psychological Review,* 1941, 356–361.

Lorenz, K. *On Aggression*. New York: Harcourt, Brace & World, 1966.

Mallick, S. K., and B. R. McCandless. A study of catharsis of aggression. 4, *Journal of Personality and Social Psychology,* 1966, 591–596.

Maslow, A. H. Deprivation, threat, and frustration. 48, *Psychological Review,* 1941, 364–366.

Miller, N. E. The frustration-aggression hypothesis. 48, *Psychological Review,* 1941, 337–342.

Miller, N. E. Theory and experiment relating psychoanalytic displacement to stimulus-response generalization. 43, *Journal of Abnormal and Social Psychology,* 1948, 155–178.

Miller, N. E. Liberalization of basic S-R concepts: Extensions to conflict behavior, motivation, and social learning. In S. Koch (ed.), *Psychology: A Study of a Science,* Vol. 2. New York: McGraw-Hill, 1959.

Miller, N. E. Some implications of modern behavior theory for personality change and psychotherapy. In P. Worchel and D. Byrne (eds.), *Personality Change.* New York: Wiley, 1964.

Moore, Shirley G. Displaced aggression in young children. 68, *Journal of Abnormal and Social Psychology,* 1964, 200–204.

Mowrer, O. H. *Learning Theory and Behavior.* New York: Wiley, 1960.

Moyer, K. E. *Kinds of Aggression and Their Physiological Basis.* Report No. 67–12. Dept. of Psychology, Carnegie-Mellon University, Pittsburgh, Pa., 1967.

Otis, N. B., and B. McCandless. Responses to repeated frustrations of young children differentiated according to need area. 50, *Journal of Abnormal and Social Psychology,* 1955, 349–353.

Pastore, N. The role of arbitrariness in the frustration-aggression hypothesis. 47, *Journal of Abnormal and Social Psychology,* 1952, 728–731.

Roberts, W. W., and H. O. Kiess. Motivational properties of hypothalamic aggression in cats. 58, *Journal of Comparative and Physiological Psychology,* 1964, 187–193.

Rothaus, P., and P. Worchel. The inhibition of aggression under nonarbitrary frustration. 28, *Journal of Personality,* 1960, 108–117.

Scott, J. P. Agonistic behavior of mice and rats: A review. 6, *American Zoologist,* 1966, 683–701.

Sears, R. R. Non-aggressive reactions to frustration. 48, *Psychological Review,* 1941, 343–346.

Seay, B., and H. F. Harlow. Maternal separation in the rhesus monkey. 140, *Journal of Nervous and Mental Diseases,* 1965, 434–441.

Spence, K. W. *Behavior Theory and Conditioning.* New Haven: Yale University Press, 1956.

Ulrich, R. Pain as a cause of aggression. 6, *American Zoologist,* 1966, 643–662.

Ulrich, R. E., and N. H. Azrin. Reflexive fighting in response to aversive stimulation. 5, *Journal of the Experimental Analysis of Behavior,* 1962, 511-520.

Yates, A. J. *Frustration and Conflict.* London: Methuen, 1962.

Zajonc, R. B. *Social Psychology: An Experimental Approach.* Belmont, Calif.: Wadsworth, 1966.

2 : *The Frustration-Aggression Hypothesis*

NEAL E. MILLER

with the collaboration of

ROBERT R. SEARS, O. H. MOWRER,

LEONARD W. DOOB, and JOHN DOLLARD

The frustration-aggression hypothesis is an attempt to state a relationship believed to be important in many different fields of research. It is intended to suggest to the student of human nature that when he sees aggression he should turn a suspicious eye on possibilities that the organism or group is confronted with frustration; and that when he views interference with individual or group habits, he should be on the lookout for, among other things, aggression. This hypothesis is induced from common sense observation, from clinical case histories, from a few experimental investigations, from sociological studies, and from the results of anthropological field work. The systematic formulation of this hypothesis enables one to call sharp attention to certain common characteristics in a number of observations from all of these historically distinct fields of knowl-

From *Psychological Review*, vol. 48, 1941, pp. 337–342. Copyright 1941 by the American Psychological Association.

edge and thus to take one modest first step toward the unification of these fields.

A number of tentative statements about the frustration-aggression hypothesis have recently been made by us in a book.[1] Unfortunately one of these statements, which was conspicuous because it appeared on the first page, was unclear and misleading as has been objectively demonstrated by the behavior of reviewers and other readers. In order to avoid any further confusion it seems advisable to rephrase this statement, changing it to one which conveys a truer impression of the author's ideas. The objectionable phrase is the last half of the proposition: "that the occurrence of aggression always presupposes the existence of frustration and, contrariwise, that the existence of frustration always leads to some form of aggression."

The first half of this statement, the assertion that the occurrence of aggression always presupposes frustration, is in our opinion defensible and useful as a first approximation, or working hypothesis. The second half of the statement—namely, the assertion "that the existence of frustration always leads to some form of aggression" is unfortunate from two points of view. In the first place it suggests, though it by no means logically demands, that frustration has no consequences other than aggression. This suggestion seems to have been strong enough to override statements appearing later in the text which specifically rule out any such implication.[2] A second objection to the assertion in question is that it fails to distinguish between instigation to aggression and the actual occurrence of aggression. Thus it omits the possibility that other responses may be dominant and inhibit the occurrence of acts of aggression. In this respect it is *inconsistent* with later portions of the exposition which make a distinction between the instigation to a response and the actual presence of that response and state that punishment can inhibit the occurrence of acts of aggression.[3]

Both of these unfortunate aspects of the former statement may be avoided by the following rephrasing: Frustration produces instigations to a number of different types of response, one of which is an instigation to some form of aggression.

This rephrasing of the hypothesis states the assumption that was actually used throughout the main body of the text. Instigation to aggression may occupy any one of a number of positions in the hierarchy of instigation aroused by a specific situation which is frustrating. If the instigation to aggression is the strongest member of this hierarchy, then acts of aggression will be the first response to occur. If the instigations to other responses incompatible with aggression are stronger than the instigation to aggression, then these other responses will occur at first and prevent, at least temporarily, the occurrence of acts of aggression. This opens up two further possibilities. If these other responses lead to a reduction in the instigation to the originally frustrated response, then the strength of the instigation to aggression is also reduced so that acts of aggression may not occur at all in the situation in question. If, on the other hand, the first responses do not lead to a reduction in the original instigation, then the instigations to them will tend to become weakened through extinction so that the next most dominant responses, which may or may not be aggression, will tend to occur. From this analysis it follows: the more that successive responses of nonaggression are extinguished by continued frustration, the greater is the probability that the instigation to aggression eventually will become dominant so that some response of aggression actually will occur. Whether or not the successive extinction of responses of nonaggression must inevitably lead to the dominance of the instigation to aggression depends, as was clearly stated in later pages of the book, upon quantitative assumptions beyond the scope of our present knowledge.[4, 5]

Frustration produces instigation to aggression but this is not the only type of instigation that it may produce. Responses incompatible with aggression may, if sufficiently instigated, prevent the actual occurrence of acts of aggression. In our society punishment of acts of aggression is a frequent source of instigation to acts incompatible with aggression.

When the occurrence of acts of aggression is prevented by more strongly instigated incompatible responses, how is the existence of instigation to aggression to be determined? If only the more direct and overt acts of aggression have been inhibited, as is apt to be the case because such acts are the most likely to be punished, then the instigation to aggression may be detected by observing either indirect or less overt acts of aggression. If even such acts of aggression are inhibited, then a different procedure must be employed. Two such procedures are at least theoretically possible. One is to reduce the competing instigations, such as fear of punishment, and observe whether or not acts of aggression then occur. The other is to confront the subject with an additional frustration which previous experiments have demonstrated would by itself be too weak to arouse an instigation strong enough to override the competing responses inhibiting the aggression in question. If the instigation from this additional frustration now results in an act of aggression, then it must have gained its strength to do so by summating with an already present but inhibited instigation to aggression. The presence of the originally inhibited instigation to aggression would be demonstrated by the effects of such summation. Thus the fact that an instigation may be inhibited does not eliminate all possibility of experimentally demonstrating its presence.

At this point two important and related qualifications of the hypothesis may be repeated for emphasis though they have already been stated in the book. It is not certain how early in the infancy of the individual the frustration-aggression hypothesis is applicable, and no assumptions are made as to whether the frustration-aggression relationship is of innate or of learned origin.

Now that an attempt has been made to clarify and to qualify the hypothesis, four of the chief lines of investigation which it suggests may be briefly considered.[6]

1. An attempt may be made to apply the hypothesis to the integration and elucidation of clinical and social data. Here the fact that certain forms of aggression are spectacularly dangerous to society and to the individual is relevant. This means that acute personality conflicts are apt to arise from the problem of

handling aggression and that the problem of aggression is apt to play an important role in shaping certain great social institutions such as the in-group as an organization against the out-group.

2. An attempt may be made to formulate more exactly the laws determining the different ways in which instigation to aggression will be expressed under specified circumstances. Some of the problems in this field are suggested by the phenomena of displacement of the object of aggression, change in the form of aggression, and catharsis of aggression.

3. An attempt may be made to secure more information concerning the other consequences which frustration may produce in addition to the instigation to aggression. Such an attempt would lead into studies of rational thought and problem solution as suggested in the classical work of John Dewey, and into studies of experimental extinction, trial-and-error learning, substitute response, and regression.[7] Work along this line of investigation may deal either with the clinical and social significance of these other consequences of frustration or with the discovery of the laws governing them.

4. An attempt may be made to improve or to reformulate the basic frustration-aggression hypothesis itself. The determination of the laws which allow one to predict exactly under which circumstances instigation to aggression may be expected to occupy the dominant, the second, the third, or some other position in the hierarchy of instigations aroused by a frustrating situation is a most important problem of this type. Another problem is the reduction of the frustration-aggression hypothesis to more fundamental principles and the more accurate restatement of the hypothesis in terms of these more basic principles. One of the steps in this direction would be to scrutinize any exceptions to the hypothesis as now formulated. Another step would involve a careful study of the early stages of the socialization of the individual in an attempt to analyze the interlocking roles of three factors: first, innate physiological reaction patterns; second, learning mechanisms; and third, the structure of the

social maze which poses the learning dilemmas and contains the rewards and punishments. An empirical and theoretical analysis along these lines might lead to a fundamental reformulation giving a closer approximation to the socially and scientifically useful truths imperfectly expressed in the present frustration-aggression hypothesis.

NOTES

1. J. Dollard, L. W. Doob, N. E. Miller, O. H. Mowrer, and R. R. Sears. *Frustration and Aggression*. New Haven: Yale University Press, 1939.
2. *Ibid.,* pp. 8–9, 19, 58, 101–102.
3. *Ibid.,* pp. 32–38; also 27, 39–50, 75–87, 111, 166. In this later exposition a distinction is made not only between instigation to aggression and acts of aggression but also between conspicuous acts of overt aggression and inconspicuous acts of non-overt aggression. It is assumed that the former are more apt to be culturally inhibited by strong punishments than the latter.
4. *Ibid.,* p. 40.
5. The notions used here are similar to those employed by Professor Hull in describing trial-and-error learning. See C. L. Hull, Simple trial-and-error learning—an empirical investigation. 27, *J. comp. Psychol.,* 1939, 233–258.
6. Both of the first two of these chief lines of investigation have been developed at length in *Frustration and Aggression*. No attempt was made there to elaborate upon either the third or the fourth. Thus that first effort does not purport to be a complete systematization of all principles within a single field, but rather, an exploratory attempt to apply a strictly limited number of principles to several different fields. *Op. cit.,* pp. 18, 26.
7. These problems are discussed in more detail by R. Sears in Non-aggressive responses to frustration. 48, *Psychol. Rev.,* 1941, 343–346.

3: *Extinction-Induced Aggression*

N. H. AZRIN

R. R. HUTCHINSON

D. F. HAKE

When shock is delivered to the feet of an animal, attack results (Ulrich and Azrin, 1962). Other unconditioned aversive stimuli such as shock to the tail (Azrin, Hutchinson, and Sallery, 1964), a physical blow (Azrin, Hake, and Hutchinson, 1965), or intense heat (Ulrich and Azrin, 1962) also cause attack. Perhaps attack will also result from aversive events other than unconditioned aversive stimuli. Evidence exists that parts of a schedule of food reinforcement are aversive. For example, immediately after reinforcement, subjects will respond to terminate a reinforcement schedule that has a high response requirement (Azrin, 1961). One aspect of rein-

From *Journal of the Experimental Analysis of Behavior*, vol. 9, 1966, pp. 191–204. Published with the permission of the authors and the Society for the Experimental Analysis of Behavior, Inc. Copyright 1966 by the Society for the Experimental Analysis of Behavior, Inc.

This investigation was supported by grants from the Mental Health Fund of the Illinois Department of Mental Health, NIMH Grant 4925, and NSF Grant 1987. T. Ayllon and J. Keller provided valuable advice and assistance.

forcement schedules that seems to have aversive properties is extinction. Several investigators have inferred the existence of a "frustrating" or "emotional" state during extinction as reflected by oscillations in the response rate (Skinner, 1938), attacking of the response lever (Mowrer and Jones, 1943), increased vocalization between children (Azrin and Lindsley, 1956), and increased running speed after omission of a food reinforcement for running (Amsel and Roussel, 1952). The most direct evidence of the aversive properties of extinction has emerged from studies (e.g., Ferster, 1958; Ferster and Appel, 1961; Baer, 1962; Holz, Azrin, and Ayllon, 1963; Zimmerman and Ferster, 1963) that have used an extinction period as a punisher for responses. Based on this evidence, the present study attempted to determine whether the aversive properties of extinction of food reinforcement could produce attack. The general rationale was to alternate periods of continuous reinforcement with periods of extinction. A subject was stationed nearby to serve as the target for any attack that might occur.

Experiment I

Method

Subjects. Eighteen experimentally naive male pigeons from one to five years of age were obtained from Palmetto Pigeon Plant, Sumter, South Carolina. Sixteen were White Carneaux, one was a Silver King, and the other was a White King. All were maintained at 80 per cent of free-feeding weight. Each experimental pigeon was paired with a target pigeon. The 18 target pigeons were White Carneaux, except for S-144, which was a White King. It was paired with the experimental White King. The target pigeons were maintained at free-feeding weight. All pigeons were housed in individual living cages with water and grit continuously available.

Apparatus. Figure 1 shows a schematic of the apparatus. At one end was a food tray located behind an aperture. Above the

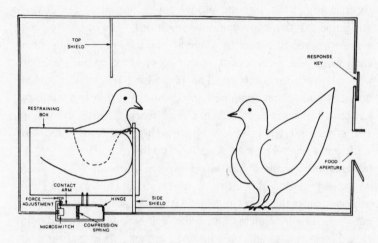

FIGURE 1. Schematic of the apparatus for measuring attack. The experimental chamber was $26 \times 14 \times 14$ inches high. Plexiglass shields at the top and on the sides of the restraining box prevented the experimental pigeon from getting behind the target pigeon.

aperture was a response key consisting of a plastic panel which was exposed through a ¾ inch diameter hole in the wall and transilluminated from behind. A response was defined as a peck on the key in excess of 20 g. Each response produced a click. Food reinforcement was delivered by raising the food tray to a level that could be reached through the wall aperture. A photocell (not shown) was mounted above the food tray so that a narrow beam of light was interrupted when the head of the pigeon was in the aperture. The duration of food reinforcement was timed by maintaining the food tray in the accessible position for 1.0 sec. from the moment of interruption. This photocell and timing arrangement was used to ensure greater control over the actual eating time. During food delivery, the lights behind the response key were extinguished and the tray was illuminated.

The apparatus for recording attack was at the other end of the chamber. Pigeons are known to fight for a variety of reasons (Levi, 1957). The apparatus was designed to provide objective measurement of attack and to reduce the "spontaneous" fighting so that attack during the study could be more definitively attributed to the experimental conditions. The target pigeon was restrained in a box by a metal band fastened snugly over each wing. The pigeon could move its head freely but the body was relatively immobilized. The restraining box was mounted on an assembly that contained an adjustable spring and a micro-switch, the contacts of which closed when a force exceeding 100 g. was exerted against the restraining box. This force was sufficient to prevent closure of the contacts by normal spon-taneous movements of the target pigeon. Closure of the switch contacts provided the measure of attack by the experimental pigeon against the target pigeon. Attack duration was measured automatically by timers. Since the contacts then opened and closed repeatedly during continued attack, their output was "smoothed" by allowing the timers to run until the contacts remained open for at least 1.0 sec. "Attack duration" refers to the smoothed output.

Closure of the switch contacts depended only partly on the force of the pecking attacks. The target pigeon characteristically moved its head vigorously when attacked in a seeming effort to escape or counteraggress. These "defensive" movements by the target pigeon plus the force of the attacking movements of the experimental pigeon caused the switch contacts to close. Visual observation indicated close correspondence between the auto-matic record of attack and visual evidence of attack as indicated by physical contact by the beak of the experimental pigeon. Occasionally, the switch contacts closed a fraction of a second before the experimental pigeon attacked, this resulting from vigorous defensive head movements by the restrained pigeon when the experimental pigeon struck with its wing or made an abortive peck from a distance before moving in. The con-tacts closed occasionally as a result of strong movements by the restrained bird in the absence of any attack; the duration of these closures never exceeded 10 sec. during any one-hour ses-sion. For one subject, the automatic recording system did not provide a valid measure of attack since the target pigeon with which it was paired adopted a submissive posture, remaining motionless and not resisting attack. The data for this subject are not included since the switch contacts did not close, even though attacks occurred.

The experimental chamber was enclosed in a sound-attenuating enclosure that contained a one-way window and a closed-circuit TV camera for continuous observation. Overhead lights in the chamber provided general illumination. White noise was presented continuously to mask extraneous sounds. A 60 cps tone, produced by a tone generator mounted within the chamber, was used as a discriminative stimulus. Programing and recording were performed automatically by circuits in an adjacent room.

Procedure

The procedure followed an ABA design consisting of no reinforcement, reinforcement-extinction, no reinforcement again. For some subjects an additional condition of reinforcement-extinction followed (ABAB). During the initial condition of no reinforcement, each experimental pigeon was given from 5–12 sessions of one-hour duration during which the target pigeon was in the restraining box but the food reinforcement mechanism was inoperative. This phase provided a measure of attack prior to any experimental history of food reinforcement.

For the reinforcement-extinction condition, the pigeons were trained to eat out of the food magazine and shaped to peck the response key. The target pigeon was not present except for one subject, S-214, which was intentionally shaped while a target pigeon was present. Each response produced the food reinforcement. This shaping procedure required one or two sessions, a maximum of 80 reinforcements being given each session. The 60 cps tone sounded continuously. From 10–20 sessions were then given in which periods of continuous reinforcement were alternated with periods of extinction, the tone serving to signal the beginning of the period of continuous reinforcement. During the first five minutes of each session, key pecks were ineffective.

After five minutes the tone sounded; the first response during the tone produced food reinforcement. The tone was terminated after this first food delivery and each subsequent response produced reinforcement until 10 were delivered, after which the key pecks were again ineffective for five minutes (extinction). Then the tone sounded, again signaling availability of food reinforcement. This cycle of reinforcement and extinction was repeated 8 times for a total of 80 reinforcements and 50 minutes of extinction during each session, excluding the first five minutes. This procedure remained in effect until responses occurred immediately upon the sounding of the tone, but few responses were made during extinction periods. The tone onset was (experimentally) delayed for five seconds by any preceding responses in order to prevent superstitious reinforcement (Skinner, 1948) of the response by the one onset.

The target pigeon was then placed in the restraining box; the alternating reinforcement-extinction procedure was still in effect. To prevent superstitious reinforcement of attack behavior, a five-second delay was imposed between occurrence of attack and onset of the tone.

A minimum of 10 sessions were scheduled, this number generally being increased whenever attack duration seemed to show a consistent change during successive sessions. At least 10 sessions were given during the second condition of no reinforcement and reinforcement-extinction. The sessions were conducted daily except when the condition of the target bird made it advisable to omit a scheduled session.

Results

Consider first the effect of the food reinforcement schedule on the key-pecking responses. The top half of Figure 2 illustrates the typical key-pecking performance in the absence of a target pigeon. The pigeons learned to peck the key within a second or two after the tone signaled the onset of the period of continuous reinforcement. Also, the pigeon pecked the response key with a short latency during the period of continuous re-

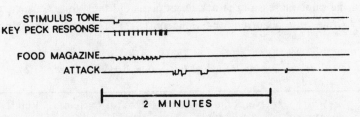

FIGURE 2. Simultaneous event recordings of the tone stimulus, the key-peck responses, the delivery of food reinforcement, and the attack against a target pigeon. A target pigeon was present during the procedure described in the lower part of the figure but not in the upper part.

inforcement; less than one second generally elapsed between termination of food delivery and the next key peck. The figure shows the characteristic burst of key-pecking responses at the onset of extinction.

The lower portion of Figure 2 illustrates key-pecking performance and attack behavior when the target bird was in the chamber. The usual burst of key pecks occurred. In addition, the pigeon attacked the target shortly after the last response of the burst. Visual observation revealed that attack consisted of strong pecks at the throat and head of the target bird, especially around the eyes. The feathers of the target bird were often pulled out and the skin bruised. The attack was often preceded by a brief period of pacing in front of the wall on which the response key was mounted. Occasionally the pecking attack was preceded by striking movements of the wing or by a slow swaying approach to the target bird with the head lowered. Frequently, the attack was preceded and accompanied by a deep-throated sound.

Table 1 shows the mean and average deviation of attack duration based on the last five days of each condition for all subjects. All pigeons attacked more during the reinforcement-extinction procedure than during the no-reinforcement procedure. The Silver King pigeon (S-78C) and White King (S-144) showed the same increase in attack duration as did the White Carneaux. Attack also occurred for the pigeon (S-214) that was magazine-

TABLE 1: *Attack During Repeated Extinction Periods—Duration of Attack (Sec)*

SUBJECT NO.	No. Reinf. MEAN	No. Reinf. AVG. DEV.	Reinf. + Ext. MEAN	Reinf. + Ext. AVG. DEV.	No Reinf. MEAN	No Reinf. AVG. DEV.	Reinf. + Ext. MEAN	Reinf. + Ext. AVG. DEV.
S-78C	3 ±	3	764 ±	86	99 ±	108		
S-111B	15 ±	8	415 ±	200	76 ±	28		
S-144	0 ±	0	105 ±	30	0 ±	0		
S-203A			353 ±	113	6 ±	5	257 ±	52
S-205	15 ±	14	1148 ±	88	5 ±	6		
S-205A	3 ±	3	157 ±	81	16 ±	13	64 +	44
S-206	12 ±	7	177 ±	130	0 ±	0		
S-208	56 ±	25	92 ±	79	2 ±	3	178 ±	70
S-209	21 ±	18	1125 ±	84	0 ±	0	734 ±	247
S-209A	10 ±	10	52 ±	35	0 ±	0	94 ±	16
S-210			38 ±	18	0 ±	0	173 ±	50
S-213	10 ±	10	254 ±	58	72 ±	42	289 ±	73
S-214	10 ±	6	456 ±	234	5 ±	5	459 ±	391
S-214A	24 ±	14	79 ±	17	16 ±	8	216 ±	50
S-218A	25 ±	10	30 ±	13	8 ±	12	65 ±	13
S-220A			223 ±	48	0 ±	0	464 ±	139
S-225	2 ±	2	288 ±	63	5 ±	5	106 ±	46

NOTE: For three of the subjects (S-203A, S-220A, and S-210) the target pigeons counteraggressed so vigorously that no aggression occurred after the first day of exposure to the reinforcement-extinction procedure. When three new target pigeons were substituted, attack occurred. These three new target pigeons were paired with the three experimental pigeons for the remainder of the experiment. No data are presented for the initial period of no-reinforcement in the first column of Table 1 for these three pigeons since those data were obtained with the different target bird.

trained and shaped to respond in the presence of the target pigeon.

Figure 3 illustrates the day-to-day changes of attack duration. The four pigeons in the figure were intentionally selected to illustrate the major intersubject differences in performance. On the first day, most pigeons had a high duration of attack, which decreased to a near-zero level on succeeding days for all pigeons. On the first day of the reinforcement-extinction procedure, duration of attack increased at least tenfold for all pigeons, thereafter declining somewhat for some, e.g., S-214A. For three pigeons, two of which (S-205, S-209) are included in Figure 3, the attack was so intense and enduring that only five sessions were given in order to prevent serious injury to the target pigeon. When the reinforcement-extinction procedure was discontinued, attack duration gradually decreased for all pigeons. When the reinforcement-extinction procedure was reinstated, the duration of attack immediately increased for all pigeons. The cumulative recordings of the attacks in Figure 4* show that attack was most likely immediately after periods of reinforcement. For most subjects it resulted after each period of food reinforcement. Often attack occurred at the very start of the session. There was no consistent change in attack as a function of session duration.

Figure 5 presents a summary of the temporal pattern of attack for eight subjects. For all subjects, attack duration was highest during the first 30 or 60 seconds after reinforcement was terminated. Thereafter, attack duration was an inverse function of the time since reinforcement, reaching a near-zero level after four minutes.

Experiment II. Omission of the Key-Peck Requirement

This experiment attempted to determine whether the key-peck response was essential for producing attack.

* Figure has been omitted in this volume.

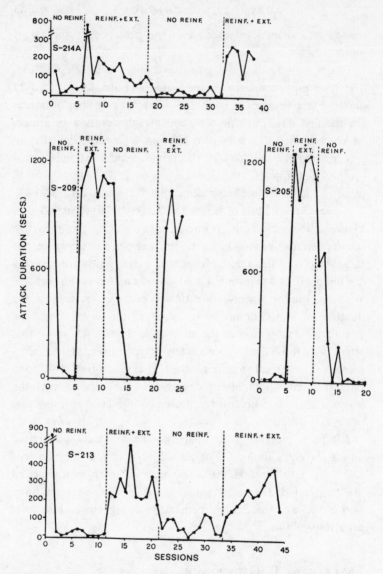

FIGURE 3. Duration of attack from the beginning of the experiment for four of the experimental pigeons. "No Reinf." designates the procedure in which no food reinforcement was delivered. "Reinf. + Ext." designates the procedure in which periods of food reinforcement were alternated with periods of extinction during each session.

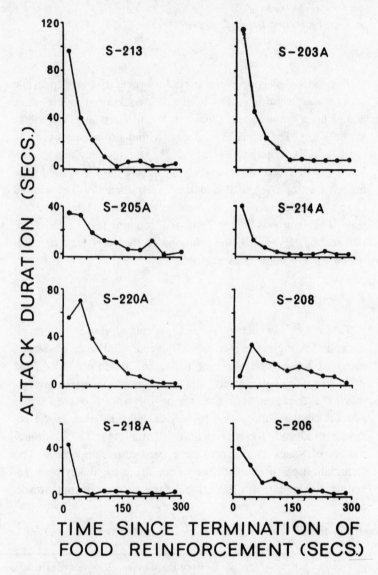

FIGURE 5. The average duration of attack as a function of time since the termination of food reinforcement. The 300 sec duration between reinforcement periods was divided into 10 30-sec class intervals. Each point designates the mean duration of attack per session during each of these class intervals for the last five sessions of the first reinforcement-extinction procedure. Each curve is for a different pigeon.

Method

Two naive pigeons were used in order to avoid possible superstitious reinforcement of the key-pecking response once it had been conditioned. One was White Carneaux, the other White King. The experimental design and procedure were the same as in Experiment I except that the response key was absent. Food was delivered automatically by raising the food tray at the instant the tone sounded and keeping it there for one second after the pigeon inserted its head into the aperture above the tray. The tone was then terminated and the tray lowered for one second. Every 10 presentations of the food tray was followed by five minutes of no food.

Results

Table 2 shows the mean and average deviation of attack duration for the two experimental pigeons. Litttle or no attack occurred when food was not delivered. When the free food deliveries were interrupted, attack duration increased several-fold. The duration of attack during this free food procedure appears comparable to that for several pigeons used in the response-produced food procedure (Table 1). The temporal pattern of attack (not shown here) was also comparable. The termination of the food delivery, not the learned key-peck response, seemed to be the critical factor in producing attack.

TABLE 2: *Attack Following Automatic Food Reinforcement—Duration of Attack (Sec)*

SUBJECT NO.	No Food MEAN	AVG. DEV.	Free Food + No Food MEAN	AVG. DEV.	No Food MEAN	AVG. DEV.	Free Food + No Food MEAN	AVG. DEV.
S-234	1 ±	2	208 ±	64	0 ±	0	1063 ±	35
S-49B	33 ±	44	386 ±	95	62 ±	21	215 ±	51

These results also show that the pecking attacks were not simply a "displacement" of the conditioned key-pecking responses.

EXPERIMENT III. SIGNALED VS. UNSIGNALED EXTINCTION

Figure 2 showed that a short period of key pecking typically occurred at the termination of food delivery during the procedure in which a key-peck was required; similarly, visual observation revealed a brief period of lingering about the food magazine at the termination of free food deliveries. These activities seemed to reflect the absence of any distinctive discriminative stimuli regarding the precise moment of transition from food reinforcement to extinction. Perhaps a more clearly defined extinction period might be less aversive, as suggested by Pavlov's observations (1927) of emotional behavior during difficult discriminations, and might not produce attack. The present procedure investigated this possibility by comparing signaled and unsignaled extinction.

Method

Two White Carneaux male pigeons were the experimental subjects; one was experimentally naive, the other (S-144) had been used in the previous procedure (see Table 1). The unsignaled extinction procedure was the same as that used previously: the tone sounded only at the onset of the period of continuous reinforcement. During signaled extinction, the tone sounded throughout the period of continuous reinforcement, terminating immediately after the last food delivery that preceded each five-minute extinction period. S-144 received at least 10 sessions under each procedure in the order described in Table 3; S-89 received only five sessions in order to prevent serious injury to its target pigeon. A key peck was required to produce the food. The signaled procedure constituted a multiple continuous reinforcement-extinction schedule (Ferster and Skinner, 1957).

Results

Table 3 shows appreciable attack during both types of extinction. S-144 attacked slightly less during the signaled than the unsignaled extinction; S-89 showed no difference perhaps because of the complications arising from injury to its target bird. Taken together, results for the two pigeons show that the onset of extinction produced attack whether or not the extinction period was signaled by a distinctive stimulus. Although unsignaled extinction produced more attack, the difference was slight.

EXPERIMENT IV. EFFECT OF A SINGLE EXTENDED PERIOD OF REINFORCEMENT AND EXTINCTION

The preceding results show that attack decreased as a function of time from the termination of reinforcement. One explanation of this relation is that attack decreased only because of some competing behavior, such as standing near the response key, that was preparatory to the onset of the next reinforcement period. The present procedure evaluated this possibility by programing only one reinforcement period during each session and by allowing a longer period of extinction.

TABLE 3: *Attack During Signaled vs. Unsignaled Extinction—Duration of Attack (Sec)*

SUBJECT NO.	Not Signaled AVG. MEAN DEV.	Signaled AVG. MEAN DEV.	Not Signaled AVG. MEAN DEV.	Signaled AVG. MEAN DEV.	Not Signaled AVG. MEAN DEV.
S-144	115 ± 57	91 ± 44	167 ± 80	82 ± 29	143 ± 58
S-89	925 ± 69	905 ± 55	797 ± 193		

Method

Two White Carneaux pigeons were studied, S-111B and S-225, both of which had been studied previously (see Table 1). The procedure was the same as the signaled extinction procedure described above, except that the period of continuous reinforcement began 30 minutes after the start of the 60-minute sessions and consisted of a single period of 60 food deliveries. Sixty sessions were given to S-111B and 40 to S-225.

Results

Figure 6 shows segments of several cumulative response records for one pigeon. It can be seen that a few instances of attack occurred before reinforcement in some of the records. During the extended period of reinforcement, little or no attack occurred. In all records, attack resulted shortly after termination of reinforcement, followed by briefer attack episodes in some cases. The second pigeon (not shown) was similar in showing little attack before reinforcement, almost no attack during reinforcement, but consistent attack at the onset of extinction. Since only one period of reinforcement was given during each session, the fall-off in attack during extinction cannot be attributed to other competing behavior associated with the onset of the next reinforcement period. The relative absence of attack during the extended food reinforcement period indicates that it is not the delivery of food, but its termination that is primarily responsible for the attack.

EXPERIMENT V. EFFECT OF SOCIAL ISOLATION FROM OTHER PIGEONS

A possible interpretation of the attack behavior is that the pigeons had an extensive history of competition over food and had been reinforced thereby for successful attack. The delivery of food simply may have reinstated the conditions for competitive attack.

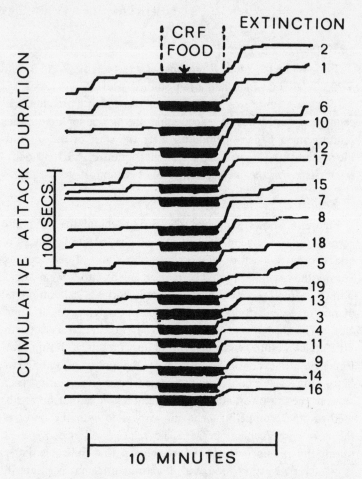

FIGURE 6. Cumulative records of the attack behavior of an experimental pigeon. The recorder pen stepped one response for every 1 sec of attack. The pen was deflected downward during each 1-sec delivery of food giving the appearance of a solid horizontal bar during the 60 food deliveries that occurred in the period of reinforcement designated as "CRF FOOD." The records are for 19 consecutive sessions. For considerations of space, the order of the 19 response records has been rearranged; the actual chronological sequence is indicated by the numbers to the right of each curve. The segments shown cover the 5-min period preceding and following the period of continuous food reinforcement. The tone that was used as a discriminative stimulus sounded throughout the period of reinforcement.

Method

The present procedure eliminated the possibility of a history of competitive attack by rearing four White Carneaux pigeons in isolation from other pigeons. If the attack behavior depended on a prior history of competition, these pigeons should show little attack. Contact with other pigeons was limited to the five-week period after hatching, during which each pigeon was alone with its respective parent bird in isolated breeding cages. Contact with the parent bird during this initial period is considered essential for survival (Levi, 1957). For nine months thereafter, they were housed in individual living cages with no possibility of physical contact with each other or with any other pigeons. Food and water were available at all times. At 10 months of age, the four pigeons were divided into two pairs, one member of each pair being designated as a target pigeon and the other as an experimental pigeon. The general procedure was the same as that described for the pigeons in Table 1.

Results

Table 4 shows that the reinforcement-extinction procedure produced substantial attack. The absolute duration was fairly comparable to that of the nonisolated pigeons used previously. The temporal pattern of attack (not shown) also was the same: attack occurred primarily at the onset of extinction. The comparability of results indicates that the attack behavior was not a result of a history of competition over food.

TABLE 4: *Attack by Socially Deprived Pigeons—Duration of Attack (Sec)*

SUBJECT NO.	No Reinf. MEAN	AVG. DEV.	Reinf. + Ext. MEAN	AVG. DEV.	No Reinf. MEAN	AVG. DEV.
S-258	2 ±	2	124 ±	33	33 ±	25
S-255	24 ±	18	290 ±	137	6 ±	9

EXPERIMENT VI. EFFECT OF FOOD SATIATION AND FOOD INACCESSIBILITY USING A MODEL AS THE TARGET

This procedure investigated which aspect of the food delivery was essential for producing attack. Did the food have to be eaten or was the mere sight of food sufficient? Stuffed pigeons, prepared by a taxidermist, were used as the target in an attempt to reduce some of the variability that seemed to arise from counteraggression by live target birds.

Method

Forty experimental pigeons were exposed to the general reinforcement-extinction procedure. The target was a stuffed White Carneaux pigeon. Only 10 of the 40 pigeons attacked the stuffed pigeon; 5 of these were selected at random to serve as subjects. The apparatus was identical to that shown in Figure 1, except that a stuffed pigeon was mounted on a stiff wire at the usual location of the live target pigeon. The wire was attached to a switch that closed when a force of 50 g. was exerted against the front of the pigeon. The sequence of procedure was: inaccessible food; food reinforcement-extinction; inaccessible food; food reinforcement-extinction; and satiation. At least five sessions were provided for each procedure. The stuffed pigeon was present throughout. During the condition of inaccessible food, the tray was covered by a thin Plexiglas shield. It was raised for one second, lowered for one second, raised again for one second, etc., for a total of 10 presentations. Five minutes then elapsed after which another 10 tray presentations were given. During the reinforcement-extinction procedure, the Plexiglas shield was removed and the food could be eaten. The satiation procedure was identical to the reinforcement-extinction procedure except that food was continuously available in the living cages.

Results

Figure 7 shows that the reinforcement-extinction procedure produced the same temporal sequence of attack as when live pigeons were used as the target. All five subjects attacked mostly within 30 seconds after termination of food reinforcement: the duration of attack again was an inverse function of the time since reinforcement. The bar graph of Figure 8 shows that the reinforcement-extinction procedure produced a substantial increase of attack for all five pigeons over the level seen when food was inaccessible or when the pigeons were satiated. These results indicate that the food had to be consumed by the pigeon if attack were to occur. No attack resulted if the pigeon was prevented from eating either by a physical obstruction or by prior satiation. The mere sight of food did not produce appreciable attack.

About 25 per cent of the pigeons attacked the stuffed target pigeons, whereas all pigeons attacked live target pigeons. The variables responsible for these individual differences have not been identified. Variations were made in the size, posture, position, and degree of movement of various stuffed target pigeons but most pigeons still would not attack. Variations were also made in the degree of food deprivation of the experimental pigeon, the age and strain of the experimental pigeon (White King, Silver King, White Carneaux), the number of food deliveries and the duration of extinction. All of these changes failed to induce consistent attack against the stuffed target. Stuffed models of birds have been used previously (cf. Smith and Hosking, 1955). If a stuffed model had elicited attack consistently in this study, it would be a more desirable type of target since the measure of attack behavior would not be confounded by spontaneous movements of the target.

EXPERIMENT VII. NUMBER OF FOOD REINFORCEMENTS

It has been seen that interruption of eating by a hungry pigeon was a prerequisite condition for producing attack. This implies that food has been delivered for some period before its termina-

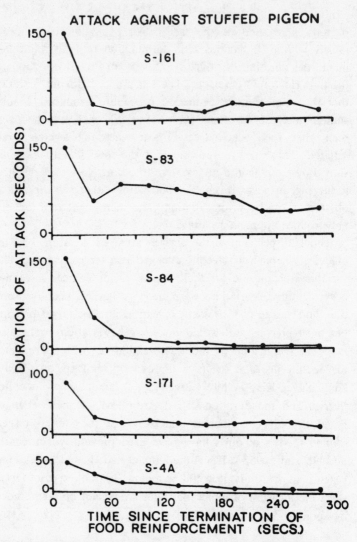

FIGURE 7. Duration of attack against a stuffed pigeon as a function of time since the termination of food reinforcement. Each curve is for a different pigeon. The 5-min duration between reinforcement periods was divided into 10 30-sec class intervals. Each point designates the mean duration of attack per session during each of these class intervals. The points are based on 10 sessions constituting the last five sessions of each reinforcement-extinction procedure.

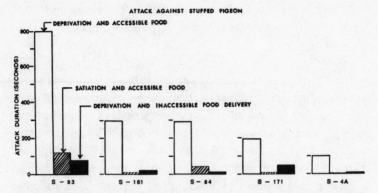

FIGURE 8. Mean duration of attack by each of five pigeons against a stuffed pigeon. Each bar in the figure shows the mean duration of attack based on the last five sessions under the designated condition. The white bar designates the condition when the pigeons were food-deprived and the food was accessible (10 sessions); the stippled bar is when the pigeons were satiated, but food was still accessible (five sessions). During this period described by the solid black bar (10 sessions), the pigeon was food-deprived, but the food was inaccessible.

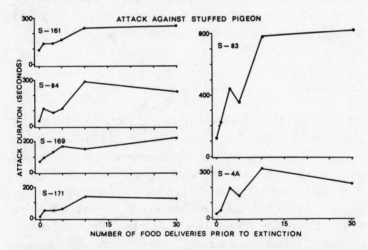

FIGURE 9. Duration of attack as a function of the number of food reinforcements that preceded extinction. Each curve is for a different experimental pigeon. Each point is the mean of the last three sessions, or five sessions when five or more were given.

tion. The present procedure attempted to determine how the number of food deliveries affected duration of attack.

Method

The same apparatus, procedure, and subjects were used as in the preceding reinforcement-extinction procedure except that a sixth subject was added and only five periods of reinforcement were given each session. Again, a stuffed pigeon served as the target. 0, 1, 3, 5, 10, or 30 food deliveries were given during each reinforcement period, at least three sessions being provided for each number in a scrambled sequence that differed between subjects. When 30 food deliveries were scheduled, sessions were conducted only on alternative days in order to maintain the pigeons at their usual reduced weight.

Results

Figure 9 shows that duration of attack was a direct function of the number of food deliveries that preceded extinction, reaching an asymptote at 10 food deliveries. The slightly reduced level of attack at 30 food deliveries for S-4A and S-84 probably was caused by partial satiation within a session.

DISCUSSION

Considerable attention was given to the methodological problems in measuring attack since progress in the study of attack will probably depend greatly on the development of satisfactory measures. Yet, the very nature of attack creates special problems for its long-term study and objective measurement. If the target is defenseless, death can result (cf. Roberts and Kiess, 1964). Conversely, if the target is capable of effective counter-aggression, attack gives way to "aggressive" postures, threats, etc., and requires subjective rating scales, as has been the case in studying attack between rats (Ulrich and Azrin, 1962) or between monkeys (Azrin *et al.*, 1964). One solution has been to use an inanimate object as the target (Azrin *et al.*, 1964; Azrin *et al.*, 1965; Azrin, Hutchinson, and McLaughlin, 1965). If one desires to study aggression between live animals, however, the pecking mode of attack of pigeons is advantageous for long-term study since it is less destructive than the usual biting attack of other animals. The problem of counteraggression by the target bird was reduced by partially restraining it. The present method of recording attack provided an objective and fairly accurate record of physical attack between two live animals over relatively long periods of time. The two main disadvantages were occasional instances of serious injury to the target bird, and the occasional target bird that counteraggressed sufficiently to discourage future attack.

For all subjects, the duration of attack was increased by the reinforcement-extinction procedure and maintained for as long as it remained in effect (over three months for some birds). The reversibility of the phenomenon was evidenced by the change in attack duration when the reinforcement-extinction procedure was discontinued, reinstated, and discontinued again.

Even casual observation of pigeons in their coops reveals fighting over food. The present results indicate strongly that the attack observed here was not attributable to competition over food. The target pigeons were restrained in a fixed location with no opportunity to compete. The two pigeons had no previous contact with each other, and the food was not delivered near the target pigeon. It also seems unlikely that the attack can be attributed to generalization from a history of competition since attack occurred for the pigeons that were raised in social isolation.

The simple sight of food and its termination were not sufficient to produce attack. The food had to be consumed. Attack did not occur when the food was not consumed either because the subjects were satiated or because the food was physically unobtainable.

A possible explanation of the attack is that it was maintained by superstitious reinforcement by the food as might be suggested by the results of Reynolds, Catania, and Skinner (1963), who used food as a reinforcer for attack between pigeons. This explanation seems inappropriate for several reasons. First, the birds were food-reinforced for several days in the absence of a target bird; yet attack usually resulted on the first day it was introduced. Second, a delay was used in the delivery of food to prevent food from being delivered shortly after an attack. Third, the post-reinforcement attack occurred even when only a single period of food reinforcement was used and no possibility existed of a food delivery after this attack. Fourth, attack very rarely occurred during a period of continuous reinforcement when the possibility of superstitious reinforcement would be greatest.

The finding (Ulrich and Azrin, 1962) that attack is produced by aversive events suggested that occurrence of attack might be a means of evaluating possible aversiveness of a schedule of food reinforcement. If a schedule of positive reinforcement is aversive, it might be expected to produce attack. Further, that aspect of the schedule that is most aversive might be revealed by identifying the moment of greatest attack. The present findings revealed a high frequency of attack at the moment of transition from continuous reinforcement to extinction. The attack decreased as a function of time from the transition. Therefore, the transition from continuous reinforcement to extinction may be considered an aversive event.

The usual procedure for ascertaining the aversiveness of an event is the escape paradigm: Will conditioning result for the response that terminates that event (Holland and Skinner, 1961; Keller and Schoenfeld, 1950)? In attempting to determine the aversiveness of a schedule of food reinforcement, this procedure requires that the subject make a response that produces a time-out from the food reinforcement procedure. The results of studies using that procedure support the present interpretation that some aspects of a schedule of positive reinforcement may be aversive (Pliskoff and Tolliver, 1960; Azrin, 1960; Azrin, 1961; Hearst and Sidman, 1961; Thompson, 1964, 1965).

Many schedules of intermittent reinforcement will probably possess aversive properties since intermittency necessarily involves periods of extinction. A major implication of the present findings is that schedules of reinforcement may produce aggression as a by-product that is not apparent when the individual is studied in isolation. In the present study, the principal effect of the extinction procedure was the burst of key-pecking responses at the onset of extinction when the subject was alone in the experimental chamber. When the target subject was also located in the chamber, it became apparent that extinction had a far greater effect than simply reducing the number of key pecks.

The present findings have been interpreted as the result of the aversive properties of extinction. Additional evidence with other reinforcers and other types of animals are needed to evaluate the generality of this phenomenon.

REFERENCES

Amsel, A., and J. Roussel. Motivational properties of frustration: I: Effect on a running response of the addition of frustration to the motivational complex. 43, *J. exp. Psychol.*, 1952, 363–368.

Azrin, N. H. Use of rests as reinforcers. 7, *Psychol. Rep.*, 1960, 240.

Azrin, N. H. Time-out from positive reinforcement. 133, *Sci.*, 1961, 382–383.

Azrin, N. H., D. F. Hake, and R. R. Hutchinson. Elicitation of aggression by a physical blow. 8, *J. exp. Anal. Behav.*, 1965, 55–57.

Azrin, N. H., R. R. Hutchinson, and R. McLaughlin. The opportunity for aggression as an operant reinforcer during aversive stimulation. 8, *J. exp. Anal. Behav.*, 1965, 171–180.

Azrin, N. H., R. R. Hutchinson, and R. D. Sallery. Pain-aggression toward inanimate objects, 7, *J. exp. Anal. Behav.*, 1964, 223–227.

Azrin, N. H., and O. R. Lindsley. The reinforcement of cooperation between children, 52, *J. abnorm. soc. Psychol.*, 1956, 100–102.

Baer, D. M. Laboratory control of thumb-sucking by withdrawal and representation of reinforcement. 5, *J. exp. Anal. Behav.*, 1962, 525–528.

Ferster, C. B. Control of behavior in chimpanzees and pigeons by time-out from positive reinforcement. 72, *Psychol. Monogr.*, 1958, No. 8 (Whole No. 461).

Ferster, C. B., and J. B. Appel. Punishment of S responding in matching to sample by time-out from positive reinforcement. 4, *J. exp. Anal. Behav.*, 1961, 45–56.

Ferster, C. B., and B. F. Skinner. *Schedules of Reinforcement.* New York: Appleton-Century-Crofts, 1957.

Hearst, E., and M. Sidman. Some behavioral effects of a concurrently positive and negative stimulus. 4, *J. exp. Anal. Behav.*, 1961, 251–256.

Holland, J., and B. F. Skinner. *Analysis of Behavior.* New York: McGraw-Hill, 1961.

Holz, W. C., N. H. Azrin, and T. Ayllon. Elimination of behavior of mental patients by response-produced extinction. 6, *J. exp. Anal. Behav.*, 1963, 407–412.

Keller, F. S., and W. N. Schoenfeld. *Principles of Psychology.* New York: Appleton-Century-Crofts, 1950.

Levi, W. M. *The Pigeon.* Sumter, S.C.: Author, 1957.

Mowrer, O. H., and H. Jones. Extinction and behavior variability as functions of effortfulness of task. 33, *J. exp. Psychol.*, 1943, 369–386.

Pavlov, I. P. *Conditioned Reflexes.* London: Oxford University Press, 1927.

Pliskoff, S., and G. Tolliver. Water-deprivation-produced sign reversal of a conditioned reinforcer based upon dry food. 3, *J. exp. Anal. Behav.*, 1960, 323–329.

Reynolds, G. S., A. C. Catania, and B. F. Skinner. Conditioned and unconditioned aggression in pigeons. 6, *J. exp. Anal. Behav.*, 1963, 73–74.

Roberts, W. W., and H. O. Kiess. Motivational properties of hypothalamic aggression in cats. 58, *J. comp. physiol. Psychol.*, 1964, 187–193.

Skinner, B. F. *The Behavior of Organisms: An Experimental Analysis.* New York: Appleton-Century-Crofts, 1938.

Skinner, B. F. Superstition in the pigeon. 38, *J. exp. Psychol.*, 1948, 168–172.

Smith, S., and E. Hosking. *Birds Fighting.* London: Faber and Faber, 1955.

Thompson, D. M. Escape from S associated with fixed ratio reinforcement. 17, *J. exp. Anal. Behav.*, 1964, 1–8.

Thompson, D. M. Punishment by S associated with fixed ratio reinforcement, 8, *J. exp. Anal. Behav.*, 1965, 189–194.

Ulrich, R. E., and N. H. Azrin. Reflexive fighting in response to aversive stimulation. 5, *J. exp. Anal. Behav.*, 1962, 511–520.

Zimmerman, J., and C. B. Ferster. Intermittent punishment of S responding in matching to sample. 6, *J. exp. Anal. Behav.*, 1963, 349–356.

4: Physical Aggression in Relation to Different Frustrations

ARNOLD H. BUSS

Most of the research on aggression during the past twenty years has been conducted in the context of the frustration-aggression hypothesis (Dollard, Doob, Miller, Mowrer, and Sears, 1939). This hypothesis assumes that frustration is the sole antecedent of aggression, and it specifies the variables determining the intensity of aggression: strength of frustration and punishment of aggression. The stronger the frustration, the more intense the aggression; the stronger the punishment (or threat of punishment), the weaker the aggression.

The present research was conducted in a different context; the position is set forth in detail elsewhere (Buss, 1961). Briefly,

From *Journal of Abnormal and Social Psychology*, vol. 67, 1963, pp. 1–7. Copyright 1963 by the American Psychological Association.

The author thanks Robert Alderisio, Rae Detwiler, Sam Freeman, Jean McCulla, and Gracia Venetos, who participated in the experiment and helped analyze data. Timothy Brock, Peter Lang, and Merle Moskowitz made helpful suggestions concerning the manuscript.

61

frustration is viewed as only one of several antecedents of aggression, and not the most potent antecedent. Concerning the relationship between frustration and aggression, the two determinants specified by Dollard *et al.* (intensity of frustration and punishment of aggression) are only part of the list. Also included are arbitrariness of aggression, type of aggression, and instrumental value of aggression.

Arbitrariness refers to the presence or abuse of justification for the frustration. When one individual's ongoing behavior is blocked because of the whimsy or petulance of another, the frustration is arbitrary. If the blocking is either necessary or beyond anyone's control, the frustration is nonarbitrary. Pastore (1952) was the first to suggest and then demonstrate that arbitrary frustration leads to more aggression than nonarbitrary frustration.

Aggression, defined as the delivery of noxious stimuli to another, may be divided into active versus passive and direct versus indirect types (Buss, 1961). In both passive and indirect aggression, it is difficult to identify the aggressor, who is therefore unlikely to suffer counteraggression. The less likely the counteraggression, the more probable the aggression. Thus frustration should elicit more frequent and intense aggression when the allowable aggression is passive and indirect than when it is active and direct.

Aggression may also be verbal or physical. In adults, verbal aggression is more frequent than physical aggression, which has been inhibited during the process of socialization. Because of this inhibition, frustration is less likely to lead to aggression when the allowable aggression is physical than when it is verbal.

The instrumental value of aggression is also important. When a child's crying and whining interfere with an adult's studying, slapping the child will usually silence him. Since the aggression overcomes the frustration in this instance, it has instrumental value and consequently a high probability of occurrence. However, if the child were very young, slapping him would elicit only more whining and crying. In this instance the aggression does not remove the interference, and, since it has no instrumental value, its probability of occurrence is low. Noninstrumental aggression occurs when the aggressor is angry and vents his anger by inflicting pain on a victim; but such aggression, since it is not reinforced by removal of frustration or acquisition of a reward, is less likely to occur than is instrumental agression.

Because of the difficulties of investigating aggression in the laboratory, there is little reliable knowledge about any of the five determinants of the frustration-aggression relationship. Surprisingly, there have been few studies in which aggression is studied in relation to pure frustration; a number of researchers have confounded verbal insult with frustration and therefore have added little to knowledge about the effects of simple frustration.

Frustration is defined here as a stimulus event: the blocking of learned instrumental or consummatory behavior. It is manipulated by establishing a goal and then interfering with the instrumental behavior leading to the goal. Little is known about the effect of blocking different motivations because task failure has been virtually the only frustration manipulation used in the laboratory.

The present experiment compared three kinds of frustration: task failure, failure to achieve a monetary reward, and a failure to achieve a better scholastic grade. Failure on a laboratory task is only a mild challenge to self-esteem, whereas not winning money constitutes a deprivation of reward, and not attaining a better grade is both a deprivation and a potential punishment (lower grade). Thus the three types of frustration may be ordered *a priori* in increasing intensity: task failure, not winning money, and not attaining a better grade. Intensity of aggression was predicted to vary with this increasing magnitude of frustration.

In predicting the intensity of aggression the other four determinants need to be considered. The frustration was nonarbitrary, which should lead to less intense aggression. The type of aggression was active and physical (the subject delivered varying intensities of electric shock to another person), which should also diminish intensity of aggression. However, the aggressor knew there would be no counteraggression, and, in the absence of punishment, aggression intensity should be high. Finally, the aggression had no instrumental value, which should diminish intensity. The instrumental value of aggression is, in the writer's view, the most important determinant of aggression. In the absence of such value, it was predicted that the intensity of aggression would be low.

METHOD

Measurement of Aggression

The apparatus is an "aggression machine" that is described fully elsewhere (Buss, 1961). The subject is brought together with another ostensible subject, and told that the two of them will participate in an experiment; this second "subject" is actually an experimental accomplice, hereafter called "the victim." The subject and the victim are told that one of them will be the experimenter and the other, the subject. Each chooses a card, and the subject always receives a card saying, "Experimenter" (actually both cards say "Experimenter," but the victim reports that his says "Subject"). This lottery procedure helps to sustain the cover story of the experiment.[1]

The subject is then taken to the experimental room and shown how to present stimuli (patterns of lights) and record responses. Whenever the victim makes a correct response, the subject flashes a "Correct" light; whenever the victim makes an incorrect response, the subject shocks him. The victim gives the same programed series of responses to all subjects, and the victim (unknown to the subject) records the intensity of each shock given.

There are 10 shock buttons, and at the start of the experiment the subject is given shock from Buttons 1, 2, 3, and 5 in order to know how much punishment he will deliver. Buttons 1 and 2 give mild shock, which increases in intensity until at Button 5 it is quite painful; the subject is told that shock intensity continues to increase through the remaining 5 buttons.

When the victim is brought in, the subject places the shock electrode on his fourth finger, explains briefly that this is a learning experiment, and then presents the stimuli of the first trial. The subject is told to shock the victim on the first 10 trials "in order to wipe out any pre-experimental response tendencies." On Trials 11–20 the victim makes six errors; on Trials 21–30 he makes five errors; and thereafter he makes four errors per 10 trials until he finally learns (five consecutive correct responses) starting at Trial 70.

The victim receives no shock because he disconnects the shock circuit with a hidden switch. In order to maintain realism, the victim gasps or groans whenever the shock is 8, 9, or 10; he gasps or groans half the time when the shock is 6 or 7.

The delivery of punishment by the subject is labeled aggression in accordance with the generally accepted definition of aggression: the delivery of painful or noxious stimuli to another organism. If the subject restricted the intensity of shock to Buttons 1 and 2, the punishment would be so minimal that it might not qualify as aggression. However, since Buttons 3 and higher deliver clearly painful stimuli, such responses are unequivocally aggressive; the subject is no longer merely informing the victim of an incorrect response, but he is delivering noxious stimuli as well.

Frustration Procedure

The subject was told that his goal was to teach the victim a concept; the mode of frustration was the relative inability of the victim to learn. Intensity of frustration was manipulated by varying the subject's incentive in getting the victim to learn quickly, on the assumption that the stronger the blocked motivation, the stronger the frustrating procedure. There were three incentives for the subject: proving his own ability to obtain learning on the task, earning money, or obtaining a better grade in a course.

Know-how. The subject was told that previous studies had established that the know-how and general intelligence of the experimenter was a major determiner of learning and that more capable experimenters were getting faster learning. The rationale was that the experimenter is in effect teaching a concept, and better teachers get faster learning. Thus the more know-how the subject possessed, the faster would be the victim's learning. The subject was told that the victim should reach criterion by about 19 or 20 trials *after the end* of the 10-trial "confusion series." If by some chance the victim did not learn by then, the subject was to keep going until he did; but slower learning was ostensibly an unlikely event.

Money. The subject was told that speed of learning was in part determined by the experimenter's ability, but this was not emphasized. He was told that in order to get people to learn as rapidly as possible, monetary rewards were being given to the fastest two-person teams (subject plus victim): $10 each to the fastest team, $5 each to the next fastest team, and $2 each for the third place team. He was told that the money came from a research grant and that while it was not much, it should give an added incentive for learning quickly. Otherwise the instructions were the same as for the Know-how group.

Grades. The subject was told that because the experiment involved teaching, learning, and general psychological skill, the introductory psychology professor was interested in the results. The results (speed of learning and therefore adequacy of the subject's teaching) would be turned over to the professor, who would use them in determining grades. Naturally, the information would not count as much as an exam, but it would be supplementary information that would help in cases of borderline grades; it would give the professor an idea of how the student performs in a psychological situation outside the classroom. Otherwise the instructions were the same as for the

Know-how group. When the experiment was over, the subject was told of the deception and that the reason for it was to motivate both members of the two-person team. This rationale was elaborated in terms of fictitious experimental and control groups, and no subject was dismissed until he was at ease concerning his grades.

Two subjects in this group reported afterward that the "grades story" had not fooled them, but their data turned out to be no different from other members of the group, and they were retained. Two subjects falsified scores, claiming spuriously fast learning; these subjects were discarded, but they provided suggestive evidence that the motivation for grades was stronger than that in the other two experimental groups. In addition, casual observation of the subjects' reactions when they were told that the results were unrelated to their grades ("Thank God," sighs of relief) suggested the presence of stronger motivation here than in the other two frustration groups.

Control. The subject was told nothing about the determiners of learning, and, unlike the subjects in the experimental groups, he was told that it would probably require 65–75 trials for the victim to reach criterion. If the subject asked why it required so many trials, he was told that the concept was more difficult than it appeared to be. As in the other groups, the victim made five consecutive correct responses (the criterion) starting at Trial 70.

Subjects

The subjects were recruited from introductory psychology classes. Three students were discarded for reasons stated above; two women refused to participate in a shock experiment; and three students misinterpreted or failed to understand instructions and were discarded. The data of 160 subjects were used in the experiment, 40 in each of the four groups. There were 20 men and 20 women in each group, and half the subjects had a male victim and the other half, a female victim.

RESULTS

During the first 10 ("confusion") trials 10 shocks were given, and in the subsequent 60 trials 26 more shocks were given. These 36 shock trials were divided into six blocks of six trials each in order to see clearly trends that might be obscured by random trial-to-trial variations. The third block of trials marks the point at which it became apparent that the victim was not going to learn quickly enough for the subject to succeed in his teaching task, and therefore any increase in aggression (shock intensity) should commence at this point.

Because of sex differences, the men's and women's data were analyzed separately. For the men the first block of shock trials varied between approximately 2.5 and 3.0, and there were no significant differences between groups for this block of trials. Thereafter the three frustration groups all increased their intensity of aggression. The Grades and Money groups had similar, steep increases, and the Know-how group showed a moderate increase. The Control group manifested very little increase in aggression through the six blocks of trials.

The significance of these trends was tested in an analysis of variance, which is presented in Table 1. The relevant slope

TABLE 1: *Analysis of Variance of Men's Data*

SOURCE	df	MS	F
Groups (G)	3	2205.3	2.4
Sex of Victim (V)	1	6969.0	7.5*
G × V	3	271.7	
Between subjects in the same group	72	925.7	
Trials (T)	5	567.6	12.2**
T × G	15	114.4	2.4*
T × V	5	55.4	1.2
T × G × V	15		
Pooled subjects × Trials	360	47.1	
Total	479		

* $p = .01$.
** $p = .001$.

statistic is the Trials × Groups interaction, which is significant beyond the .01 level. Pair-by-pair comparisons of the curves revealed that all three Frustration curves were significantly steeper than the Control curve, and the Know-how curve was not significantly flatter than the Grades curve, but was flatter than the Money curve at the .05 level. Thus, for the most part, the predicted difference between Know-how, Money, and Grades failed to materialize.

The other important finding in the men's data was a sex difference for victims. Male subjects administered significantly more aggression to men than they did to women.

Inspection of the women's data indicates that for the first block of shock trials the groups ranged from 2.0 to 2.5; as with the men, these small and random differences were not statistically significant. Although the Control group started at a slightly higher level than the Frustration groups, its rise was very slight. The three Frustration groups showed a steady rise throughout the six blocks of trials.

The appropriate analysis of variance is presented in Table 2. Again the Trials × Groups interaction is significant at the .01 level, and again frustration clearly leads to aggression. The women's data show no differences between the Frustration groups; the curves of the three experimental groups are sim-

TABLE 2: *Analysis of Variance of Women's Data*

SOURCE	df	MS	F
Groups (G)	3	109.7	—
Sex of Victim (V)	1	1.0	—
G × V	3	350.0	—
Between subjects in same group	72	627.0	
Trials (T)	5	1988.4	52.6**
T × G	15	108.5	2.9*
T × V	5	28.2	—
T × G × V	15	35.5	—
Pooled subjects × Trials	360	37.8	
Total	479		

* p = .01.
** p = .001.

ilar throughout the six blocks of trials, and all three are significantly steeper than that of the Control group.

Comparing the male and female data, it is clear that the men's curves are higher than the women's. An analysis of variance was performed on the men's and women's data combined. It was found that the men were significantly more aggressive than the women (F = 10.0, p < .001, df = 1/144). Furthermore, there was a significant Subject × Victim interaction (F = 4.2, p < .05, df = 1/144); men aggressed significantly more against men than against women, but women did not.

Discussion

Because the frustration was nonarbitrary and the allowable aggression was active, physical, and noninstrumental, it was predicted that frustration would lead to only minimal aggression. The results confirm the prediction. The increase in shock level was slight, averaging 1.5 units in the frustration groups; this was only 1 unit more than the increase of the controls.

It was also predicted that the Know-how, Money, and Grades groups would be ordered in terms of increasing aggression. This prediction was only partially confirmed for men and not at all for women. In general, frustrations of apparently different intensities did not lead to different intensities of aggression. There are two explanations of this finding.

First, the frustrations may not have been of different intensities. There have been no published data concerning the relative strengths of various frustrating procedures, and in the absence of such data, we cannot be sure that frustrations of apparently different intensities really are different. Nevertheless, according to frustration-aggression theorists (Dollard *et al.*, 1939) one way of varying the strength of frustration is to vary the strength of the motivation being blocked. The three goals in the present study were: success as an experimenter, acquisition of a moderate sum of money, and securing a good grade or at least not a bad one. These were ordered *a priori* in increasing order of motivational strength. While there is no laboratory evidence to sustain this assumption, it seems reasonable in light of what is known about college students. If the motivations did differ in strength, it follows that the frustrations differed in intensity.

It may be argued that the subjects should have been asked how frustrated they were. There are two objections to this. First, this argument implicitly defines frustration as a reaction of the organism, whereas frustration has already been defined as a blocking manipulation. Such equivocation would lead to: frustration (blocking) leads to frustration (emotional state). The circularity of this statement is the consequence of defining frustration in two entirely different ways, a confusing state of affairs.

Of course the definition of frustration as a stimulus event might be discarded for the alternative definition of frustration as a reaction of the organism. This leads to the second objection. What does a subject mean when he says, "I feel frustrated"? He might mean anxiety, mild depression, anger, or something as vague as being upset; or he might mean all of these. Not only does the term *frustration* have different "internal" referents, but it is a difficult task for anyone to describe accurately or quantitatively something as vague as a "feeling of frustration."

As a last resort, the subject might be asked to rate the intensity of his anger. Although this was impractical in the present study (see the Method section), it might be done in similar experiments. Such a rating would constitute a second dependent variable, measuring the emotional reaction that often accompanies aggression. However, it would be a measure of the success of the frustration manipulation only if frustration were defined as an event that always leads to anger. Since no one defines frustration this way, such a self-report would tell us nothing about the intensity of frustration.[2]

It is assumed, on the basis of casual observation of everyday behavior, that there were differences in the strength of the motivation of the subjects in the Know-how, Money, and Grades groups. It follows from the reasoning of Dollard *et al.* (1939) that there were differences in intensity of frustration. Since corresponding differences in aggression were generally absent, we may question whether aggression intensity covaries with frustration intensity.

The second explanation concerns this very issue: the covariation of frustration and aggression. Frustration does not always lead to aggression, a point conceded by one of the authors of the frustration-aggression hypothesis (Miller, 1941). Frustration may result in the seeking of other means of reaching the goal or giving up the goal, at least temporarily; or it may elicit emotional reactions such as anxiety or depression.

When a strong motivation is blocked, the frustration is intense. The intense frustration may lead to marked anxiety or depression but not necessarily to intense anger (the "instigation to aggression" of the frustration-aggression hypothesis). Thus a more intense frustration might lead to more intense nonaggressive reactions but only mild aggression. It is believed that this is precisely what occurred in the present experiment.

The results, so interpreted, cast doubt on a corollary of the frustration-aggression hypothesis, namely, that the intensity of aggression covaries with the intensity of frustration. This corollary has received support only in questionnaire studies in which subjects indicated how angry or aggressive they *would be* in frustrating situations (Allison and Hunt, 1959; Doob and Sears, 1939). There has been no laboratory confirmation of the hypothesis, and its present status may best be described as unproven.

It should be remembered that in the present experiment aggression was valueless in overcoming frustration; however, there are situations in which aggression is successful in overcoming the interference. When aggression is instrumentally valuable, the stronger the motivation being blocked (and therefore the stronger the frustration), the more intense should be the aggression. The hypothesis being offered is that the instrumental value of aggression determines the frustration-aggression relationship. When aggression has no instrumental value, its intensity is unrelated to that of frustration; when aggression has instrumental value, its intensity covaries with the intensity of frustration.

The sex difference in aggression intensity was consistent with the results of pilot studies with the "aggression machine" and with widely held beliefs: the men were more aggressive than the women. The novel sex difference was the subject-victim interaction: the men aggressed more against men than against women, but the women aggressed equally against men and women. While no one will be surprised by this result, it may well be that with other kinds of aggression (indirect or verbal aggression) different subject-victim interactions will be found. In any event, the data suggest that in research on aggression the sex of the target may be as important as the sex of the aggressor.

A final comment concerns the paradigm used here. It is one solution to the ethical and practical problems of investigating aggression under controlled conditions, and it yields quantitative and repeated measures of physical aggression. The findings in the present study, with aggression as the dependent variable, as well as those in a previous study in which aggression was the independent variable (Brock and Buss, 1962), suggest that it is a potentially useful research technique.

NOTES

1. The lottery procedure was suggested by Stanley Milgram.
2. Two types of experiments may be distinguished. In the first type (S–R) a dependent variable is studied in relation to an independent variable, and it is necessary only to: specify the experimental (stimulus) operations, and show that they meet the definition of the independent variable. Thus in the present study aggression (delivery of a noxious stimulus) was studied in relation to frustration (block-

ing of learned behavior leading to a goal). It sufficed to describe the blocking manipulations (operational definition), and it would be irrelevant to inquire about the success of the manipulation. The only relevant question was: what is the relationship between frustration and aggression?

In the second type of experiment (S–R–R) a dependent variable is studied in relation to a response or state of the organism that is itself the result of a manipulation, e.g., the effect of guilt on attitude change. In such a study there would be a manipulation designed to make the subject guilty. The independent variable is guilt, not the manipulation, and therefore the success of the manipulation must be determined. Assessment of the success of the manipulation yields an estimate of guilt; once the degree of guilt is known, it may be related to the dependent variable (attitude change). In this type of study the independent variable, being the organism's reaction, is assessed *after* the experiment has been conducted. In the first type the independent variable, being a manipulation or stimulus event, is known and specified *at the start* of the experiment.

REFERENCES

Allison, J., and D. E. Hunt. Social desirability and expression of aggression under varying conditions of frustration. 23, *J. consult. Psychol.,* 1959, 528–532.

Brock, T. C., and A. H. Buss. Dissonance, aggression, and evaluation of pain. 65, *J. abnorm. soc. Psychol.,* 1962, 197–201.

Buss, A. H. *The Psychology of Aggression.* New York: Wiley, 1961.

Dollard, J., L. W. Doob, N. E. Miller, O. H. Mowrer, and R. R. Sears. *Frustration and Aggression.* New Haven: Yale University Press, 1939.

Doob, L. W., and R. R. Sears. Factors determining substitute behavior and the overt expression of aggression. 34, *J. abnorm. soc. Psychol.,* 1939, 293–313.

Miller, N. E. The frustration-aggression hypothesis. 48, *Psychol. Rev.,* 1941, 337–342.

Pastore, N. The role of arbitrariness in the frustration-aggression hypothesis. 47, *J. abnorm. soc. Psychol.,* 1952, 728–731.

5: *Arbitrariness of Frustration and Its Consequences for Aggression in a Social Situation*

EUGENE BURNSTEIN

PHILIP WORCHEL

The generality of the frustration-aggression hypothesis as set forth by Dollard, Doob, Miller, Mowrer, and Sears (1939) has been challenged by such findings as those of Pastore (1952), Cohen (1955), and Rothaus and Worchel (1960). These investigations have shown that frustrations which are perceived to be reasonable or nonarbitrary are accepted with much less overt aggression than those which are perceived to be arbitrary or unreasonable. This reduction in overt aggression may be due to a decrease in the instigation to aggression or to the arousal of inhibitory forces. Rothaus and Worchel found evidence supporting the latter alternative of response inhibition under arbitrary frustrations.

From *Journal of Personality*, vol. 30, 1962, pp. 528–541. This research was supported in part by the United States Air Force under Contract No. AF 49(638)-460 monitored by the AF Office of Scientific Research of the Air Research and Development Command and, in part, by the University of Texas Research Institute.

75

All of the above studies, however, utilized questionnaires in presenting frustrations to Ss. With this method, the reduction in the frequency of aggressive responses under nonarbitrary frustration could result from factors other than the nature of the frustration (e.g., response sets, social desirability considerations, etc.). Hypothetical frustrations are not likely to attain the intensity of real frustrations and therefore the social pressures to respond with impunity to reasonable (nonarbitrary) frustrations may far outweigh any hypothetically aroused aggressive tensions.

It was considered necessary, therefore, to replicate the studies of Pastore (1952) and Rothaus and Worchel (1960) under experimental conditions, and to determine whether, given such conditions, the reduction of aggression under nonarbitrary frustrations is due to response inhibition or to a decrease in the instigation to aggression. If it is due to response inhibition, then, following Miller's (1948) theory of displacement, (a) there should be greater displacement of aggression under nonarbitrary than arbitrary frustration, and (b) reducing the strength of the inhibitory forces postulated under nonarbitrary frustration should lead to an increase in direct aggression and to a decrease in indirect aggression (displacement). On the other hand, if the reduction of aggression is a result of the lowered instigation to aggression, then manipulating the strength of the social norms postulated to inhibit the expression of aggression should not affect the degree of direct or indirect aggression.

METHOD

Subjects

One hundred male Ss selected from the different sections of the introductory course in psychology participated in the present experiment. They served in small groups of 3 to 5 Ss each. No group contained more than one S from any particular section. By serving as Ss they fulfilled a course requirement.

Instigation Procedures

All groups were given "The Case of Johnny Rocco" to discuss under three different conditions of frustration: (a) arbitrary frustration, (b) nonarbitrary frustration, and (c) no frustration. In all three conditions, when the Ss had seated themselves about a table they were addressed by E somewhat as follows:

You are to be some of the first students to participate in a program of evaluating the conference group skills of undergraduates at the University. Such skills reflect important basic abilities and the University would like to know how each student stands in respect to these abilities. In the first phase of testing a person's conference skills, we in the psychology department have decided it would be best to bring together a small group of undergraduates, to present them with a type of discussion problem that commonly confronts conference groups and see how well they handle it. In a minute you are each going to receive a sheet, the top half of which will contain a section of the case history of a boy, Johnny Rocco. Each of you will have a different section of the case history. Some will have material on his family, another will have material on his school life, and so on. On the bottom half of the sheet each of you will have the identical material. It is a paragraph outlining the current problem which confronts Johnny Rocco. When you read the bottom paragraph you will note that a decision must be made about what course of action should be taken with this boy. Your group is to pool the various bits of information it has about the case history, discuss the case, and in the light of the discussion arrive at a decision as to what is the best course of action to take with Johnny Rocco in the problem that confronts him. Since this is a *test* of how well you perform as a group we have placed two important restrictions on the discussion. First you will have a limited time to discuss the problem and decide on a solution. After I leave the room you will have 15 minutes to carry out and complete the discussion. Second, since we are interested in the group product, the course of action you decide on must be one which is acceptable to each and every member of the group before you can consider that a solution has been reached. This is important to remember. The decision you make must be a *unanimous* one. If no decision is reached within 15 minutes or if the decision is not unanimously acceptable then the group is considered to have failed the discussion problem. Thus, one of the most important aspects of the solution is reaching unanimous agreement about what course of action to take with Johnny Rocco. Each member of the group will receive a conference skill score that directly depends on how well the group has done on the discussion problem.

Nine groups of *S*s served under each condition of frustration: arbitrary, nonarbitrary, and control (no frustration). The same confederate participated in all sessions. His function was to delay the two experimental groups so that they would fail to reach a unanimous decision within the allotted time. To make the experimental conditions comparable, it was important that his delaying tactics be as closely alike as possible in all sessions. In the arbitrary situation, however, his behavior would be perceived as willful and unnecessary, and in the nonarbitrary condition as reasonable and not under his control.

Arbitrary frustration. In this situation, the confederate frequently asked members to repeat or clarify a point. He would interrupt with "What did you mean?" or "What did you say?" or "Do you think that's important?" At other times, he would remark, "I don't understand" or "I don't follow you" or "I don't see why we have to do this." At no time was he to engage in arguments or take any strong position about the case. His frequent interruptions delayed the group so much that a unanimous solution could not be reached within the prescribed time limits.

Nonarbitrary frustration. In groups run under this condition the confederate appeared as an *S* wearing a hearing aid.* After *E* left the room, the confederate complained that his hearing aid had broken and requested that the members explain what

* Appreciation is expressed to Mrs. H. R. Mayhall, Beltone Hearing Service, Austin, for the loan of the hearing aid.

the situation was all about since the instructions were not at all audible to him. He manipulated the hearing aid frequently in order to hear better. Throughout the discussion he requested many repetitions and clarifications (as in the arbitrary condition), often requiring other members to write out what they wished to communicate to him. Therefore, the confederate, through no fault of his own but because of an apparent failure in his hearing aid, acted to hinder the discussion in such a fashion that a unanimous decision could not be reached within the 15-minute period.

No frustration. In this condition the confederate was present but did not act to hinder the discussion. He played the role of the average member, attempting not to contribute too much nor too little to attaining a unanimously acceptable solution within the given interval.

To assure a high degree of consistency in the behavior of the confederate under all conditions, several "dry runs" were conducted for practice and to test the realism of the "interruptions." In addition, all groups were observed behind a one-way mirror by one of the *E*s to note any serious deviations in the prescribed role of the confederate and to observe the behavior of the *S*s toward the frustrating agent. Since the instructions for all groups were identical, it was assumed that the drive to complete the task successfully was the same for all sessions. Objectively the frustration was also similar in that all groups, under the two experimental conditions, failed to attain the goal. Therefore, differences in aggression for the frustrated groups would presumably have to be attributed to factors other than intensity of frustration or primary instigation (blockage of goal attainment).

For all groups, *E* re-entered the room after 15 minutes to announce that the time was up and to inquire if a unanimous solution had been reached. Under both conditions of frustration, *E* expressed surprise that agreement was not reached since the vast majority of the groups in previous sessions were able to form such a solution. In the no-frustration condition, *E* expressed satisfaction over the group's ability to decide on a course of action since previous groups had a rather difficult time and many of them had failed.

Rejection Conditions

In all conditions, it was announced that another session of testing would be given at a later date. The test would involve a very similar discussion problem. Members were then given an opportunity to vote on which of the other Ss they would prefer to be in the group at the next session and which Ss they would prefer to be replaced by another person in the pool of Ss to be tested. Within each condition of frustration three subconditions of rejection were introduced. Three groups of Ss were randomly assigned to each condition of rejection. These subconditions differed in the degree to which social pressures existed to inhibit rejection.

Public rejection. Each S sat in front of a card containing a letter "A," "B," "C," etc. The E called out each letter in order. If a member wished to reject the person designated by the letter he was to raise his hand when the letter was called. E pointed out that if a majority of the members voted to reject a particular S he would be replaced and would receive a lower "conference skill score" than the rest of the group because rejection indicated incompetence on the part of the rejected member. It was assumed the rejection under such conditions would be strongly inhibited by social norms and internalized standards prescribing the public expression of clearly hostile acts.

Private punitive rejection. A sheet of paper was distributed to each S along with a cover sheet. On the upper section of the sheet the Ss recorded the letters of the member they wished to retain; on the lower section they recorded the letters of the members they wished to reject. The E stressed that the cover sheet be held as much as possible over the voting sheet in order to assure that the vote be completely private. The Ss were informed before voting that rejection by a majority of members implied a lack of abilities and would cause the rejected S to receive a lower "conference skill score" than the rest of the group. It was here assumed that a privately expressed hostile act would be subjected to less inhibition from norm pressure than a public one. The only inhibiting force would stem from internal standards regarding aggression against arbitrary or non-arbitrary agents of frustration.

Private nonpunitive rejection. The procedure was similar to that followed in the punishment condition except for the following: (a) Ss were told that often certain individuals disrupted or hindered discussion in one group but performed with efficiency in another, and (b) groups often find from experience that they would carry out a discussion with much more harmony and efficiency if one or more members were replaced by other individuals. This was said to be quite common. It was stressed that any person rejected by the group would in no way be penalized. He would be placed in another group and a new member would appear in his place at the next session. Furthermore, it was pointed out this may be to the benefit of the member who does not perform well in the present group, for he may excel in a different group setting. It was assumed that the least amount of inhibiting pressure from norms and internal standards existed against rejection under such conditions.

Measures of Displacement

Following a vote all Ss were asked to fill out a questionnaire designed to assess their negative feelings about themselves (S) toward the confederate (C) and toward E by encircling the appropriate category following each item (except the last three items). The items with the scoring categories indicating the object of aggression in parentheses are as follows:

(S)   1. To what degree did your action interfere with the progress of the group? (1-none of my actions interfered to 6-all of my actions interfered)

(E)   2. In your opinion, how competent was the psychologist who conducted the experiment in which you just participated? (1-extremely competent to 6-extremely incompetent)

(E)   3. What is your reaction now to the psychologist who

conducted the study in which you just participated? (1-I like him very much to 6-I dislike him intensely)

(S) 4. Was it hard for you to concentrate on this test? (1-no, it was extremely easy to concentrate, to 6-yes, it was extremely hard to concentrate)

(S) 5. Would you have done better if the examiner had not been present? (1-no better to 6-extremely much better)

(S) 6. Do you get anxious when participating in such a test? (from 1-not at all to 6-extremely anxious)

(E) 7. Do you think the examiner would make a good instructor? (from 1-an excellent instructor to 6-very poor instructor)

(S) 8. Did you feel adequate in participating in this test? (from 1-very adequate to 6-very inadequate)

(E) 9. Do you think the examiner is an intelligent person? (from 1-very intelligent to 6-below average)

(S) 10. Did you have any difficulty in understanding the instructions on the test? (from 1-no difficulty at all to 6-a great deal of difficulty)

(E) 11. Do you think the testing procedure was fair and reasonable? (1-extremely fair to 6-extremely unfair)

(C) 12. Make an estimate of the academic grade-point average of each member.

(C) 13. Rank members in terms of whom you like best.

(C) 14. Rank order members in terms of their contributions to the solution of the problem.

Following the completion of the experiment all Ss were given a full explanation of the hypotheses and procedure.

RESULTS

Indices of hostility toward the confederate are presented in Tables 1, 2, and 3. In Table 1 the percentage and number of Ss who rejected the confederate under the various conditions of frustration are shown. Many more Ss voted to replace the confederate under the arbitrary condition (24 Ss) than in the nonarbitrary (8 Ss) or no-frustration (0 Ss) situation. When the condition of rejection is considered, the number of Ss voting the confederate out of the group increased considerably from the public to the private nonpunitive situation. Under the arbitrary frustration, 100 per cent of Ss rejected the confederate in both private situations. Under nonarbitrary frustrations, however, the percentage of Ss rejecting the confederate increased as the punitiveness and the visibility of the vote decreased: from 0 per cent in the public situation, to 27 per cent in the private-punitive, to 50 per cent in the private-nonpunitive situation.

On the questionnaire concerning the attitude and feelings toward the confederate, the differences between the two experimental situations were not significant (Tables 2 and 3). On "contribution to task," 6 per cent of the Ss in the arbitrary frustration and 3 per cent in the nonarbitrary frustration ranked the confederate above the median. On "members they liked best," only one S (3 per cent) in the arbitrary situation and only 3 Ss (10 per cent) in the nonarbitrary situation ranked the confederate above the median. In the control or no-frustration condition, over 40 per cent ranked the confederate above the median in "contribution to task" and "liking." Similar results were obtained on estimated academic grade-point average. Table 3 shows that the confederate received a significantly lower grade-point average in the two frustrating conditions than in the no-frustration situation, but there were no significant differences between the arbitrary and nonarbitrary frustrations (6.71 and 6.62, respectively).

Mean evaluation of hostile reactions to E and self derived from the questionnaire are presented in Table 3. The F ratios for the condition of frustration on both indices are significant beyond the .01 level. Since greater displacement of aggression was predicted for the nonarbitrary condition, one-tailed t tests were used to compare the means of the two frustration conditions on the examiner and self scores. In both cases, aggression was significantly higher at less than the .05 level toward the

TABLE 1: *Percentage and Number of Ss Who Reject Confederate Under Various Conditions of Frustration and Rejection*

	Arbitrary (N = 34)		Nonarbitrary (N = 33)		No Frustration (N = 33)	
	%	NO.	%	NO.	%	NO.
Public	29	4	0	0	0	0
Private-punitive	100	11	27	3	0	0
Private-nonpunitive	100	9	50	5	0	0
		24		8		0

TABLE 2: *Percentage and Number of Ss Ranking Confederate Above Median for "Contribution to Task" and "Liking" Under Various Conditions of Frustration*

	Arbitrary (N = 34)		Nonarbitrary (N = 33)		No Frustration (N = 33)		Chi-Square
	%	NO.	%	NO.	%	NO.	
Contribution	6	2	3	1	42	14	22.13*
Liking	3	1	10	3	45	15	22.80*

* p < .01.

examiner and self (t of 1.97 and 2.22, respectively). To test the hypothesis that reducing the postulated social pressures inhibiting the expressing of aggression in the nonarbitrary condition would reduce the tendency to displace, mean ratings of aggression toward E were calculated separately for each condition of expression—that is, public, private punitive, and private

TABLE 3: *Mean Evaluation of Negative Attitudes on Examiner and Self Items, and the Estimated Grade-Point Average ($A = 1$ to $F = 11$) of Confederate Under the Various Conditions of Frustration*

	Arbitrary			Nonarbitrary			No Frustration		
	PUBLIC ($N = 14$)	PRIV-PUN ($N = 11$)	PRIV-NONPUN ($N = 9$)	PUBLIC ($N = 12$)	PRIV-PUN ($N = 11$)	PRIV-NONPUN ($N = 10$)	PUBLIC ($N = 10$)	PRIV-PUN ($N = 13$)	PRIV-NONPUN ($N = 10$)
Examiner									
2	2.60	2.09	2.24	3.12	2.36	2.65	1.65	1.98	1.34
3	2.26	2.27	1.90	3.17	2.84	2.07	2.11	2.06	2.36
7	2.43	2.51	2.49	3.23	2.51	2.74	1.79	1.95	1.80
9	2.51	2.01	2.51	2.75	3.04	2.81	2.04	2.33	2.56
11	2.25	2.19	2.22	3.38	2.85	2.69	2.06	2.13	2.09
Mean	2.41	2.21	2.27	3.13	2.72	2.59	1.93	2.09	2.03
Self									
1	2.07	2.08	2.24	2.61	1.94	2.19	1.24	1.69	1.38
4	2.19	2.53	2.37	2.85	2.96	2.80	2.10	2.07	2.17
5	2.10	1.37	1.62	2.94	2.63	2.57	1.12	1.04	1.09
6	3.13	3.08	3.20	3.75	3.60	3.29	2.68	2.92	2.07
8	2.45	2.63	2.53	2.68	3.12	2.84	2.53	2.23	2.18
10	2.64	1.93	1.96	2.33	2.67	2.39	2.20	1.76	1.68
Mean	2.43	2.27	2.32	2.86	2.82	2.68	1.98	1.95	1.76
Conf. (Grade)	6.21	8.72	5.02	6.70	5.83	7.39	2.35	2.51	2.46
Mean (Examiner)	2.31			2.83			2.02 ($F = 17.05$)		
Mean (Self)	2.35			2.79			1.90 ($F = 10.63$)		
Mean (Conf.)	6.71			6.62			2.45 ($F = 21.27$)		

nonpunitive. These means were 3.13, 2.72, and 2.59, respectively. The mean difference between the public and private punitive was significant at the .02 level. Comparable differences were not obtained, as inspection of Table 3 reveals, when self-aggression is considered.

DISCUSSION

Four indices of aggression toward the confederate were obtained in the present experiment. One index, voting the confederate out of the group, significantly differentiated the two frustration groups in the direction that seems to support the conclusions of Pastore (1952), namely that the modification of an arbitrary frustration in the direction of nonarbitrariness reduces the aggressive response. This difference in aggression under the two conditions of frustration could be due to at least three factors: (a) an increase in the instigation to aggress by the apparent obnoxious behavior of the arbitrary agent over and above the frustration itself, (b) reduction in the aggressive drive in the nonarbitrary situation, or (c) inhibition of aggressive responses aroused by the "deafness" (and helplessness) of the confederate in the nonarbitrary condition.

Obnoxiousness might often be involved in arbitrariness but it is still necessary to isolate its effect. This could be accomplished by varying frustration and holding obnoxious behavior constant; that is, in the present experiment, replicating the conditions of the arbitrary situation but permitting the group to complete the task successfully.

The hypothesis that such reduction in aggression is due to a diminution in the instigation to aggress is not supported by the results on the other three indices. Contribution to task, liking, and estimated grade-point average failed to yield significant differences between arbitrary and nonarbitrary frustration, although both of the frustrating conditions yield more hostility toward the frustrating agent than the no-frustration condition.

These results, of course, seem more in line with our prediction that there are basically no differences in the instigation to aggress between the two frustrating conditions—only differences in response inhibition. However, the items evaluating ability and contribution may not necessarily reflect hostility. It would seem unreasonable to maintain that the deaf confederate contributed significantly to the task or that he is to be liked any more than the other Ss in the group. In our culture one would expect the "underdog" to arouse sympathy and protective feelings without those exposed to him necessarily maintaining that he is brighter and would make better grades than the others. In the no-frustration group the confederate was more productive, did contribute to the task, and, therefore, would be higher in the liking scale.

Voting the confederate out is a much more direct and unequivocal expression of aggression than ranking a confederate low on contribution to task, liking, or estimated grade-point average. The vote represents unqualified acceptance or rejection. Thus, the occasion for direct and absolute rejection of the "deaf" confederate (nonarbitrary frustration) may arouse strong guilt feelings confounded by sympathy for the deafness of the confederate. It would help to understand the nature of the effect of nonarbitrariness more clearly if sympathy could be isolated. In the questionnaire by Pastore (1952), sympathy was undoubtedly aroused for the repairman who did not have an article repaired at the appointed time due to a death in his family or for the girl who broke the date because of illness. On the other hand, sympathy does not seem to be a factor in the item "You are waiting at the right corner for a bus. You notice that it is a special on its way to the garage." Item analysis might have revealed the significance of sympathy although the frustrated drives differ in intensity.

The hypothesis that the reduction of aggression under nonarbitrary frustration is partly due to response inhibition is supported by the results on (a) the effects of experimentally reducing the strength of the inhibitory social pressures against expressing aggression, and (b) the displacement of hostility toward *E* and self. As the visibility and punitiveness of voting the confederate out of the group were diminished, the frequency of rejection increased in both frustration conditions. The influence of public voting was markedly evident in the arbitrary situation, where over 70 per cent of *S*s were reluctant to express their rejection even when the frustration was definitely unreasonable. When the vote was privately recorded, even with punitive consequences, all the *S*s were then able to express their rejection. When norm pressures are strong (public voting), public expression of hostility, even when justified, is markedly inhibited. In the nonarbitrary frustration, rejection of the confederate increased gradually but never equaled the level of rejection in the arbitrary situation. As discussed earlier, this difference may have been due to the continued influence of strong opposing pressures from internal standards aroused by the direct nature of the question. Perhaps projective techniques would have been more successful in decreasing the strength of the inhibitory force and would have brought the two frustration groups closer together in the frequency of aggressive response. Rothaus and Worchel (1960) were successful in demonstrating the influence of inhibitory tendencies in the nonarbitrary situation by the use of a "third person" technique.

Evidence for the influence of response inhibition was found in the expression of hostility toward *E* and self. If aggression is inhibited, it is likely that displacement would occur toward other targets (Dollard, *et al.,* 1939). In the present experiment, more hostility was expressed toward *E* in both situations of frustration than in the control situation. In line with our hypothesis, however, significantly greater hostility was expressed toward *E* under non-arbitrary frustration (where aggression toward the agent of frustration was somewhat inhibited) than under arbitrary frustration. The differences might still have been greater if a peer figure were used as *E* rather than a professor since stronger avoidance-tendencies for expressing aggression were probably aroused by the authority figure (Cohen, 1955).

The displacement of hostility under nonarbitrary frustration could be rationalized by the *S*s since the *E* was partly responsible for selecting a deaf member to participate in the group. The conception that displacement, when it does occur, is not toward *innocent* targets but those who could be viewed as frustrating agents has been advanced by Worchel (1960).

Not only was there more aggression displayed toward *E* in the nonarbitrary situation but there was also significantly greater aggression toward the self. It does seem somewhat irrational to blame oneself for failure to complete the task when the responsible person (deaf confederate) is rather obvious. However, in their study, Kregarman and Worchel (1961) also found that under conditions of reasonable or nonarbitrary frustration there was a greater tendency to express aggression toward the self.

Finally, reducing the social pressure for expressing aggression in the nonarbitrary situation did lead to lowered displacement of aggression toward *E* as predicted by a response-inhibition hypothesis. Of course, it is possible that the greater expression of hostility toward *E* was not displacement but a direct response to the rather "unfair" request by *E* that the *S*s should express their rejection publicly.

SUMMARY

It was the purpose of the present investigation to test under experimental conditions whether the reduction in aggressive responses under nonarbitrary as compared to arbitrary frustration is due to response inhibition or lowered instigation to aggression. If it is due to response inhibition, then decreasing the strength of the postulated inhibitory forces for expressing aggression should result in greater direct aggression and lower indirect aggression (displacement). Manipulating the strength of the postulated inhibitory forces should have no effect on direct or indirect aggression if the reduction of aggression under nonarbitrary frustration is due to lowered instigation to aggression.

One hundred male Ss selected from the different sections of the elementary course in psychology served in small groups of three to five Ss. All groups were given "The Case of Johnny Rocco" to discuss under three different conditions of frustration: (a) arbitrary, (b) nonarbitrary, and (c) no frustration. Within each condition of frustration, three subconditions of rejection were introduced. These conditions differed in the degree to which social pressures existed to inhibit the rejection.

The results showed that:

1. There was no significant difference in the private expression of negative feeling toward the confederate on the questionnaire between the experimental groups but both groups were significantly more negative than the no-frustration group.

2. With a decrease in the strength of the inhibiting social norms there was an increase in direct aggression (rejection of confederate) in both the arbitrary and nonarbitrary conditions, although the level of direct aggression was generally lower under the latter condition.

3. There was significantly greater displacement of aggression toward the E and the self under nonarbitrary than under the arbitrary frustration.

4. Decreasing the strength of the postulated inhibitory forces for expressing aggression under nonarbitrary frustration resulted in lesser displacement of aggression toward the E.

The above results support the hypothesis that the reduction of aggression under nonarbitrary as compared to arbitrary frustration is partly due to response inhibition.

REFERENCES

Cohen, A. R. Social norms, arbitrariness of frustration, and status of the agent of frustration in the frustration-aggression hypothesis. 51, *J. abnorm. soc. Psychol.*, 1955, 222–226.

Dollard, J., L. W. Doob, N. E. Miller, O. H. Mowrer, and R. R. Sears. *Frustration and Aggression.* New Haven: Yale University Press, 1939.

Kregarman, J. J., and P. Worchel. Arbitrariness of frustration and aggression. 63, *J. abnorm. soc. Psychol.*, 1961, 183–187.

Miller, N. E. Theory and experiment relating psychoanalytic displacement to stimulus response generalization. 43, *J. abnorm. soc. Psychol.*, 1948, 155–178.

Pastore, N. The role of arbitrariness in the frustration-aggression hypothesis. 47, *J. abnorm. soc. Psychol.*, 1952, 728–731.

Rothaus, P., and P. Worchel. The inhibition of aggression under non-arbitrary frustration. 28, *J. Pers.*, 1960, 108–117.

Worchel, P. Hostility: Theory and experimental investigation. In B. Willner (ed.), *Decisions, Values, and Groups*, Vol. I. New York: Pergamon Press, 1960.

6: A Study of Catharsis of Aggression

SHAHBAZ KHAN MALLICK
BOYD R. McCANDLESS

Many of those interested, theoretically or practically, in personality theory, therapy, or general social psychology, for that matter, believe that aggressive acting-out behavior reduces aggression and hostility. Most theory of play therapy is still based on this hydraulic notion: the frustrated, angry, hostile child behaves aggressively, and this aggressive behavior reduces his level of hostility and aggression. Many parents and teachers accept the dictum that it is well to allow their children to blow off steam. Boxing, wrestling, and other intramural athletics are considered by some to provide catharsis

From *Journal of Personality and Social Psychology,* vol. 4, 1966, pp. 591–596. Copyright 1966 by the American Psychological Association.

The authors are extremely grateful to Arthur Oestreich, director of the University Schools, Bloomington, Indiana; Lawrence Read, superintendent of schools, the Bloomington Metropolitan School System; and the principals and teachers of the three elementary schools in which the present research was conducted for permission to carry out the research, and for their cooperation in its conduct. Special thanks are due to the studies' sixth-grade confederates and third-grade subjects.

92

for hostile aggression (Miller, Moyer, and Patrick, 1956). Freud spoke of Thanatos or a death instinct constantly working to return the organism "to the quiescence of the inorganic world" (Freud, 1959, p. 108). Libido interacts with the death instinct, neutralizing its effect on the person, by directing it outward as destruction, mastery, and will to power, concepts which may be subsumed under the general term *catharsis*.

Dollard, Doob, Miller, Mowrer, and Sears (1939) consider that inhibiting aggression is frustrating, and that aggressive behavior reduces the instigation to aggression (is cathartic in its effects). Buss (1961) also believes that violent aggression (and perhaps any violent activity) diminishes anger level following frustration and results in feelings of satisfaction about the acting-out behavior. Similarly, Berkowitz (1962) argues that a person whose anger has been aroused will tend to express it and that this expression will give him feelings of satisfaction similar to those obtained upon completing any motivated task.

The research evidence about some form of counteraggression or catharsis as an aggression-reducing behavior is neither voluminous nor convincing. Thibaut and Coules (1952) find that subjects prevented from responding to the experimenters' confederate reduced friendly expressions toward the confederate significantly less than for subjects who were allowed to respond, and that those who were delayed in response increased in hostile responses more than those allowed to respond immediately.

Feshbach's (1955) well-known study using college students as subjects suggests that fantasy aggression may be cathartic. Hornberger (1959), in a partial replication of Feshbach's study, failed to obtain similar results. In another paper, Feshbach (1956) used children as subjects, and failed to find that aggressive free play reduced aggression: indeed, the boys (but not the girls) in his study who were initially low in aggressive behavior showed a significant increase in overt hostility after a series of permissive free-play experiences.

Hokanson (1961), like Feshbach (1955) and Hornberger

(1959), used college students as subjects. His 80 male subjects were studied according to whether they were high or low in "test hostility," threatened or not threatened by the experimenter with retaliation, and frustrated or not frustrated. A variety of measures were employed, of which number and vigor of aggressive *behavioral* responses made toward the experimenter and *ratings* of hostility toward the experimenter are most relevant for the present study.

Hokanson's subjects gave both more numerous and more vigorous "shocks" to the experimenter following frustration, but the more vigorous the shocks given, the less hostility they rated themselves as holding toward the experimenter following their "punishing" him. Hokanson thus finds that frustration increases *behavioral* aggression, using at least one measure similar to the one employed in the present study, and has a subfinding suggesting that behavioral expressions of aggression to the frustrater reduce or are at least associated with less intense verbal ratings of hostility toward him.

HYPOTHESES

Their interest in frustration-aggression-catharsis theory led the authors to set up and test the following five hypotheses, using children as subjects:

1. Angry aggression directed toward an inanimate object is not cathartic.

2. Aggression, unmotivated by anger or hostility, has no cathartic effect but may, instead, lead to an increase in aggressive responses, particularly in a socially permissive atmosphere.

3. Positive and reasonable verbal interpretation of a frustrating situation to the subject who has been frustrated has cathartic value in that it reduces hostility toward the frustrater.

4. Verbal aggression against a frustrater of the same sex does not reduce the hostility toward him (does not serve as catharsis).

5. United States girls, presumably because of cultural forces, will show less open aggression than boys. (a) However, in a permissive situation where privacy is assured, sex differences in open expression of aggression will be reduced.

Three experimental studies, the first a pilot study, the third an almost exact replication of the second, were conducted to test these hypotheses.

STUDY I

Methods and Results

In the first study, 30 male and 18 female children from 2 third-grade classes in a middle- and lower-middle-class public school were selected randomly from the total third-grade population and assigned randomly, 5 boys and 3 girls to each of 6 treatment conditions. Their ages ranged from 8 years, 4 months, to 9 years, 5 months, with a mean of 9 years.

Two sixth-grade children, one boy and one girl, were selected as confederates by nomination by class teachers and the school principal as "the most cooperative and dependable children in their grade." They were taken into the experimenter's full confidence.

The study followed a $2 \times 3 \times 2$ factorial design. There were 2 treatments—frustration and nonfrustration—and 3 types of interpolated activities: shooting a play gun at different targets on which were drawn figures either of a boy, girl, man, woman, cat, or dog; shooting at targets blank except for a bull's-eye; and solving simple arithmetic problems. The boy-girl dimension formed the third facet of the design.

The first phase of the study lasted for 5 minutes. In the frustration condition, the sixth-grade confederate "inadvertently and clumsily" prevented the subject from completing any of 5 moderately simple block-construction tasks. The experimenter had promised the subject a nickel for each task completed within a time limit. The confederate also interspersed his interference with a predetermined set of 6 sarcastic remarks, such as "Ha! I see! You really need money. Let's see how you get it." No subject was allowed to complete any task.

In the nonfrustration condition, the confederate (always the same sex as the subject) helped subjects to complete their tasks (all subjects were allowed to complete all tasks), and no reward was promised or given, other than the experimenter's verbal comment, "Very good," at the end of each task.

The second, or activity interpolation phase, immediately followed the treatment phase and lasted for 8 minutes.

In the third phase, each subject was shown his partner (the same-sex confederate), who was sitting outside the experimental room with his hands in contact with electric wires which were apparently attached to a shock apparatus installed in the experimental room. The experimenter casually reminded each subject in the frustration condition of the confederate's uncooperative behavior, and told him that he could "get even" by pushing a button, thus administering shocks (which would not hurt the frustrater very much, but would make him uncomfortable). They were further told that the frustrater would not know who was shocking him. No limit was set on the number of "shocks" that could be administered. The number of shocks ostensibly given to the confederate was taken as a measure of his hostility.

Subjects in the nonfrustration treatment were also shown the confederate, no mention of noncooperation was made, but they were told they could administer shocks if they wanted to and that the confederate would not know who had shocked him.

At the end of the study, the nature of the experiment was discussed with all subjects. Without exception they thought it funny.

A large number of subjects made a response of one shock only, but only a few gave a large number. The distribution of scores was thus extremely skewed, and a log $(X + 1)$ transformation of scores was used.

The analysis of variance of the transformed aggression

scores is shown in Table 1. Frustrated subjects manifested greater hostility than nonfrustrated subjects, but neither the sex of the subject nor the type of interpolated activity resulted in differences in amount of hostility.

STUDY II

Method

Thirty male and female third graders from a school with a principally middle- and upper-class population were randomly selected from third-grade classes and randomly assigned to 5 experimental conditions, 6 boys and 6 girls to each condition. Confederates were 6 boys and 6 girls, nominated as cooperative and dependable by their teachers and principal. Each worked with 5 subjects of the same sex, completing one unit of the 5 experimental conditions. As in Study I, they enjoyed the experimenter's full confidence.

The experimental tasks and the subjects' frustration or nonfrustration by the same-sex confederate were similar to those in Study I, except that subjects were given 5 nickels in advance. One nickel was taken from him after he had "failed" each of the 5 tasks, so that he ended the 8-minute frustration period penniless. At the end of this phase, each subject was asked to check a simple 5-step "like-dislike" scale ranging from 1, "I like

TABLE 1: *Analysis of Variance of the Transformed Aggression Scores in Study I (Five Boys and Three Girls in Each Condition)*

Source	df	MS	F
Frustration (F)	1	1.15566	15.10*
Activities (A)	2	.16679	2.18
Sex (S)	1	.00153	< 1
F × A	2	.07398	< 1
F × S	1	.00306	< 1
A × S	2	.24056	3.14
F × A × S	2	.12031	1.57
Error *MS*	36	(.07651)	

* $p < .01$.

him/her very much," to 5, "I really don't like him/her [the confederate] at all."

The second 8-minute experimental phase for one group each of frustrated and nonfrustrated subjects consisted of shooting guns at a target on which was placed a picture of an 11-year-old child of the same sex. The second pair of groups (one frustrated, one nonfrustrated) engaged in social talk (moderately standard for all subjects) with the experimenter for 8 minutes. The third frustration group was administered social talk plus interpretation (beginning in the third minute of conversation) to the effect that the frustrater was sleepy, upset, and would probably have been more cooperative if the subject had offered him 2 of the 5 nickels. At the end of the second phase, each subject was again asked to check the 5-point like-dislike rating of his/her confederate.

Phase 3 of Study II lasted for 2 minutes. Each subject was shown a "response box." He was told that the experimenter would go to an adjoining room and ask the confederate to do the same set of block-building tasks the subject had done. The subject could slow the older sixth grader's work by pushing one button, or help him by pushing the other. He could not push the button more than 20 times, although he need not count, as the experimenter would flash a signal light after the twentieth push. The experimenter then left the room, presumably to work with the confederate. The hostility criterion (aggression score) was the number of times the "slowing" button was pushed.

Upon completion of Study II, all subjects were told the nature of the experiment and, like the subjects in Study I, thought it great fun. Table 2 is a schematic representation of Study II.

Results

Table 3 summarizes the analysis of variance of the aggression scores (number of pushes of the slowing button). Scores were

TABLE 2: *Schematic Presentation of the Design of Study II*

1st phase (8 min.) INITIAL TREATMENT	PLAY WITH GUNS AND TARGETS		2nd phase (8 min.) SOCIAL TALK		REINTER-PRETATION		3rd phase (2 min.) MEASURE OF RESIDUAL HOSTILITY
	Boys	Girls	Boys	Girls	Boys	Girls	
Frustration	6	6	6	6	6	6	
Nonfrustration	6	6	6	6	0	0	

transformed into log scores, using a log $(X + 2)$ transformation. Only the treatments effect was significant.

Multiple comparisons were made among the total aggression scores of subjects in the different treatments, using Duncan's multiple-range test. The results of these comparisons are given in Table 4. Mean aggression scores for the aggressive play and social talk treatments did not differ significantly from each other either for the frustrated or nonfrustrated subjects. However, for each of these treatments, frustrated subjects had significantly higher mean aggression scores than comparable treatment groups of nonfrustrated subjects. These results are in line with those of Study I, where the frustration effect was highly significant, but the effect of interpolated activities was not.

Comparisons involving the interpretation group reveal that subjects to whom interpretation of the confederate was given produced significantly fewer aggression responses than subjects in the other two frustration groups (p's for each of the two

TABLE 3: *Analysis of Variance of Aggression Scores among the Experimental Conditions of Study II*

Source	df	MS	F
Treatments (T)	4	1.11387	9.49*
Sex (S)	1	.03049	1
T × S	4	.02982	1
Error MS	50	(.11739)	

* $p < .01$.

comparisons are less than .001), but this frustration group did not differ significantly from either of the two nonfrustration groups.

Like-dislike ratings, collected at the end of the first and second phases of Study II, are available for only 50 subjects. The first of these ratings was intended to reveal hostility engendered by frustration as opposed to nonfrustration, while it was hoped that the second rating would reflect the influence of the interpolated activity on attitude toward the confederate. The authors are doubtful about the success of their methods, since the correlation betwen the posttreatment and the postinterpolation rating was .90. For this reason, detailed tabular presentations of the two ratings and changes from the first to the second are not given. However, the following findings appeared:

For the first rating, F for the frustration treatment was highly significant. (The three frustration groups disliked their same-sex confederates much more than the two nonfrustration groups,

TABLE 4: *Multiple Comparisons among Total Aggression Scores of the Experimental Treatments of Second Study II*[a]

Treatments	Frustration-reinterpretation	Nonfrustration-social talk	Nonfrustration-aggressive play	Frustration-aggressive play	Frustration-social talk
Mean aggression scores	6.37391	6.52881	8.14602	13.40896	13.72438
Order	a	b	c	d	e
Multiple comparisons					
	a	b	c	d	e
a	—	ns	ns	**	**
b		—	ns	**	**
c			—	*	*
d				—	ns
e					—

a N = 6 per cell in each treatment.
* p < .005.
** p < .001.

but there were no differences among the three frustration or the two nonfrustration groups.) Fs for sex and Frustration $\times$ Sex were also significant at the .05 level of confidence. Girls admitted to less dislike than boys, but only in the frustration condition.

The pattern was the same (as would be expected from the high correlation between the two ratings) for the rating following the interpolated activity. However, when change scores were computed, F was highly significant for treatments, but not for sex or Treatments $\times$ Sex. Subjects in the social talk and aggressive play interpolated condition did not reduce their dislike of their same-sex confederate, while those in the interpretation condition did (p for each comparison was less than .005). This finding is even more striking when the high correlation between the two ratings is considered.

As has been mentioned, the authors hoped the second like-dislike rating would reflect residual hostility affected by different interpolated treatments following frustration. As such, these ratings should be correlated with the behavioral aggression score (number of times the slowing button was pushed). This proved to be the case, as the second like-dislike rating and the aggression score correlated .51.

However, it is possible that the way in which the like-dislike ratings were introduced affected the behavioral expression of aggression. Study III was run to introduce the attitudinal measures as an independent variable.

STUDY III

Study III is an exact replication of Study II in terms of procedures and number, sex, and social classes of subjects except that like-dislike ratings were administered to only half the subjects in each treatment condition and omitted for the other half.

As in Study II, raw aggression scores (slowing button pushing) were transformed into log scores using log $(X + 2)$ transformation. A $2 \times 2 \times 5$ analysis of variance was performed (*treatments*—frustration, nonfrustration—*replications*—where Replication 1 did not include like-dislike ratings, and Replication 2 included the ratings as described for Study II—and *interpolated activities*—as in Study II). Table 5 summarizes this analysis of variance.

TABLE 5: *Analysis of Variance of Aggression Scores among the Experimental Conditions in Study III*

Source	df	MS	F
Treatments (T)	4	1.0292	16.44**
Sex (S)	1	0.1986	3.17
Replications (R)	1	0.3640	5.81*
T × S	4	0.0679	1.08
T × R	4	0.1753	2.80*
S × R	1	0.0002	1
T × S × R	4	0.2297	3.67*
Error MS	40	0.0626	

* p < .01.
* p < .05.

Fs for treatments, replications, the Treatments × Replications interaction, and the triple-order interaction of Treatments × Sex × Replications were all significant. Total aggression scores for subjects who had been administered the like-dislike ratings were significantly greater than those of subjects who had *not* been given the ratings, suggesting that the x variable of being "asked to consider your enemy" may actually intensify the expression of aggression toward him. Main effects of sex and interactions of treatments and sex, and sex and replication condition were not significant.

Comparison of the broad pattern of findings of Study II with Study III reveals no significant differences in any dimension, despite the larger number of significant Fs in Study III. Hence, conclusions drawn from Study III may be considered to agree closely with those of Study II (or vice versa).

An interesting difference between the correlations of the second like-dislike ratings and the aggression scores for the two studies appears, however. For Study II, this *r* was .51, but for Study III it was —.01 (where N = 30). Of course, this may well be a chance variation. As in Study II, correlation between the first and second like-dislike ratings was high (.85 in Study III).

Discussion

One of the hypotheses toward which the three studies reported in the main body of this paper were directed questioned the value of expression of aggression as a catharsis serving to reduce (in this case, frustration-produced) aggression or hostility. This doubt appears to have been justified, at least when expression of aggression is toward inanimate objects.

Another hypothesis suggested was that aggression without anger lacks cathartic value, but that aggressive play in the presence of a permissive adult may lead to increase in aggression. All three of the studies reported above support this hypothesis. Actually, nonfrustration-aggressive play subjects consistently showed higher aggression scores (as manifested by "shocking" or "slowing down" a same-sex confederate) than nonfrustration-social talk subjects. (The difference, however, was significant only when the behavioral expression of aggression was preceded by like-dislike ratings of the experimenter's confederates.)

Taken together, the findings suggest that aggressive play, with or without previous frustration, has no cathartic value.

A major thesis of the present paper is that reasonable, positive interpretation of the frustrating situation has a cathartic effect. Studies II and III, where the hypothesis was tested, strongly support it. Behavioral expressions of aggression were lower for frustrated subjects to whom interpretations had been given, and greater reductions in "dislike" ratings occurred following interpretation.

Verbal expression of aggression (like-dislike ratings) seems to have no cathartic effect on aggression directed toward a frustrater. If anything, such an expression by rating appears to have the opposite effect. The finding, if repeated in other contexts and for other populations, has rather startling implications: Verbal expressions of hostility (in this case, ratings) may actually lead to an increase of aggressive behavior toward the subject of the hostile expression—can malicious gossip induce aggressive action? Will expression of hostile feelings in therapy lead to aggressive behavior in real life?

There were, somewhat to the authors' surprise and despite their hypothesis, no significant sex differences in behavioral expression of aggression toward frustraters. In other words, in a permissive situation where they are assured they cannot be detected, girls behave just as aggressively as boys. However, girl subjects gave more favorable like-dislike ratings of their frustraters than boys. (This finding was statistically significant in Study II, but not in Study III.) This is contrary to the general conviction that girls *talk* (in this case, *rate*), while boys *act*. The finding may, of course, be due to the ages of the subjects, most of whom were 8- or 9-year-olds. Cultural stereotypes of what is sex appropriate may not be well established by these ages, although there is considerable literature suggesting the contrary.

REFERENCES

Berkowitz, L. *Aggression: A Social Psychological Analysis.* New York: McGraw-Hill, 1962.
Buss, A. H. *The Psychology of Aggression.* New York: Wiley, 1961.
Dollard, J., L. W. Doob, N. E. Miller, O. H. Mowrer, and R. R. Sears. *Frustration and Aggression.* New Haven: Yale University Press, 1939.
Feshbach, S. The drive reducing function of fantasy behavior. 50, *J. abnorm. soc. Psychol.,* 1955, 3–11.
Feshbach, S. The catharsis hypothesis and some consequences of interaction with aggressive and neutral play objects. 24, *J. Personality,* 1956, 449–462.

Freud, S. *Beyond the Pleasure Principle*. New York: Bantam Books, 1959.

Hokanson, J. E. The effects of frustration and anxiety on overt aggression. 62, *J. abnorm. soc. Psychol.*, 1961, 346–351.

Hornberger, R. H. The differential reduction of aggressive responses as a function of interpolated activities. Paper read at American Psychological Association meeting, Cincinnati, Ohio, September 4, 1959.

Miller, F. A., J. H. Moyer, and R. B. Patrick. *Planning Student Activities*. Englewood Cliffs, N.J.: Prentice-Hall, 1956.

Thibaut, J. W., and J. Coules. The role of communication in the reduction of interpersonal hostility. 47, *J. abnorm. soc. Psychol.*, 1952, 770–777.

7

Some Conditions Facilitating the Occurrence of Aggression after the Observation of Violence

RUSSELL G. GEEN
LEONARD BERKOWITZ

An increasing body of experimental research has demonstrated that the observation of violence can increase the likelihood of subsequent aggression (Bandura, Ross, and Ross, 1961, 1963; Berkowitz, 1965a; Lovaas, 1961; Walters *et al.,* 1962). A good deal has yet to be learned, however, as to how this type of influence arises and what conditions govern the occurrence of the postobservation aggression. Witnessed violence can undoubtedly produce changes in the strength of inhibitions against aggression, as has been suggested by a number of writers (Bandura and Walters, 1963; Wheeler and Caggiula, 1966). Thus, according to several experiments conducted at the University of Wisconsin (Berkowitz and Rawlings, 1963; Berkowitz, Corwin, and Hieronimus, 1963; Berkowitz, 1965b),

From *Journal of Personality,* vol. 35, 1967, pp. 666–676.

This experiment was carried out as part of a research program sponsored by NSF Grant G-23988 to LB. RGG was primarily responsible for the design and conduct of the study.

the audience's attitude toward the observed event may regulate the subsequent aggression by affecting inhibitions against this behavior. In addition to this type of effect, the stimulus properties of the potential targets must also be considered (Berkowitz, 1964, 1965a; Berkowitz and Geen, 1966, 1967; Geen and Berkowitz, 1966). The aggressive tendencies elicited by the film violence apparently lead to the strongest attacks on persons who are associated with the victims of the observed aggression.

The emotional state of the observer is also important. Although some studies have obtained significant film effects with nonangered subjects (e.g., Walters *et al.,* 1962), the Wisconsin experiments have consistently found that the aggression-heightening consequences of observed violence are detectable only when the subjects had previously been angered by the person they are later to attack. The existing anger toward the available target-person evidently facilitates the effects of the film violence; theoretically, the anger energizes the aggressive responses and probably also produces a lowering of inhibitions against aggression in the immediate postobservation situation.

Emotion arousal could also arise from frustrations and we here inquire into the consequences of nonaggressive frustrations. Berkowitz (1962, 1965a) has advanced a modified frustration-aggression hypothesis. According to this view, the aggressive predisposition does not give rise to aggressive actions unless appropriate cues are present in the situation. Aggression cues are stimuli associated with the frustration source and/or with aggressive behavior generally. Such stimuli presumably elicit the aggressive responses the frustrated individual is ready to make. Where Buss (1961, 1966) has argued that a non-attacking frustration is not a primary determiner of aggression, the present position holds that the blocking of goal-directed behavior does increase the likelihood of an aggressive response providing there are the appropriate aggression cues and inhibitions against aggression are weak.

Witnessed violence could well affect the relation between

frustration and aggression. If a frustrated observer sees what he believes is justified aggression and then has an opportunity to attack someone associated with the victim of the witnessed aggression, his restraints against aggression would be weak and he would have encountered a target with relatively strong aggressive cue properties. As a result, he should exhibit stronger attacks against this available target than (a) someone seeing the same event who had not experienced the prior frustration, or (b) someone else for whom the available target does not have a high cue value for aggression.

Method

Subjects, who were run singly, were 108 male undergraduates enrolled at the University of Wisconsin. The experimenter met *S* and an experimental confederate posing as another subject at the experimental room and introduced them to each other by their last names only. The confederate was always presented as "Mr. Anderson." The two men were then informed by the experimenter that the experiment was designed to test the effects of punishment on learning and that one of them would eventually be given the task of learning a set of relationships. Punishment for failures in the learning task would be electric shocks administered by the other subject.

The experimenter then gave the two men small jigsaw-type puzzles, with the explanation that he wished to test their ability "to form spatial patterns out of their individual parts." This was said to be a test closely related to the relationship-learning problem to follow. The puzzle task actually served to introduce one of three treatments. In every case the confederate was given a puzzle which he was able (after pre-experimental practice) to put together. One-third of the subjects received a puzzle which, although looking like the one given to the confederate, was actually insoluble. The men were informed that they had five minutes to complete the puzzles. At the end of that time, the experimenter returned and picked up the puzzles, remarking that one of them (the confederate) had finished his but that the other (the subject) had not. At no time during this procedure did the confederate seek to interact with the subject; he spoke only when spoken to and treated the subject in a neutral manner throughout. The subject, therefore, was given a frustrating task, in the sense that he could not finish the puzzle (*Task Frustration condition*). This frustration is not an "attack" according to the strict definition employed by Buss (1961, 1966); the confederate does not deliver noxious stimuli to the subject in any direct fashion. However, he implicitly represents an attack on the subject's self-esteem since he completed the task and the subject failed to do so.

Another third of the subjects were given the same insoluble puzzle and allowed five minutes to work on it. In this condition, however, the confederate, after successfully completing his puzzle, approached the subject with amusement over his inability to succeed. The confederate told the subject that he was doing his puzzle wrong and that it was probably too difficult for him. When the experimenter returned, the confederate made several disparaging remarks about the subject's lack of ability and boasted about his own skill at problem solving (*Insult condition*). This treatment obviously combines both task frustration and an insulting verbal attack upon the subject.

A final third of the subjects were given puzzles which could be solved easily in five minutes. The confederate treated the subject in the same neutral manner as in the *Task Frustration* condition. This will be referred to as the *Control* condition.

After completing the puzzles, the subject and confederate were told they would witness a short motion picture, on the pretext that it contained information later to be used in the learning task. The film shown was either that of a violent prize fight or a one-mile foot race (Berkowitz and Geen, 1966). Half of the subjects viewed each film.

Immediately after the conclusion of the film the experimenter gave each man a mood questionnaire. This questionnaire directed the respondent to indicate his present emotional state by placing a check at the appropriate places on ten 7-point scales each anchored by polar adjectives.[1] The only scale to yield significant findings was NOT ANGRY—ANGRY. These findings will be reported; the remaining scales will not be referred to again. After picking up the completed mood questionnaires, the experimenter asked the two men for their first names, ostensibly to label their sheets appropriately. In half of the conditions the confederate identified himself as "Kirk Anderson," while in the other half he called himself "Bob Anderson."[2]

At this point the experimenter explained that all of the necessary preliminaries were over and that the learning task was to begin. The apparatus used in this part of the experiment was an "aggression machine" patterned after that originally designed by Buss (1961).

The experimenter arbitrarily designated the confederate as the person who would attempt to learn the stated set of relationships and the subject as the "teacher" who would present to the confederate both information necessary for learning and punishment for failure. After seating the subject at the control panel in the experimental room, the experimenter left the room with the confederate, explaining that he would return after the confederate had been set up in an adjoining room. The experimenter then returned to the subject and handed him a sheet containing a set of 20 random combinations of the letters A through E taken two at a time. The experimenter instructed S to present information to the confederate by pushing buttons on his panel labeled A through E according to the combinations on the list. S was told to wait until the confederate made a response and to punish incorrect responses by shocking the other man. Shocks were to be given by means of one of 10 buttons which ostensibly governed 10 shock levels of increasing intensity. Choice of intensity was left to S's discretion.

The confederate then proceeded to give 12 wrong responses out of the 20 trials, according to a prearranged schedule. The subject's choices of shock intensity were observed by the experimenter and recorded, along with the total duration (in thousandths of a minute) of the 12 shocks. The experimenter then returned to the subject and gave him a final questionnaire on which S was asked to state his degree of acceptance or rejection of the confederate on a set of 7-point scales.[3] Finally, the experimenter explained the experimental ruse to the subject, introduced the subject to the confederate, and asked the subject whether he had seen through the deception at any point.

RESULTS

Effectiveness of the Experimental Manipulation. The effectiveness of the Task Frustration-Insult manipulation was ascertained by analysis of responses to the mood questionnaire item on which the subjects rated the degree to which they felt angry. Mean ratings of reported anger are given in Table 1.

TABLE 1: *Degree of Felt Anger Reported by Subjects*

| | Boxing Film | | Track Film | |
	KIRK	BOB	KIRK	BOB
Control	3.67_{abc}	3.00_{abc}	2.11_c	2.44_{bc}
Task Frustration	4.00_{ab}	3.56_{abc}	3.67_{abc}	3.11_{abc}
Insult	3.67_{abc}	3.78_{abc}	4.22_a	3.89_{ab}

Means having different subscripts are significantly different from each other at the .05 level of confidence by a Duncan Multiple Range Test. $N = 9$ in each condition.

As this table indicates, subjects in the Task Frustration and Insult conditions tended to report themselves as being angrier than did the subjects in the Control condition. The analysis of variance of these data yielded a significant main effect of the arousal treatments ($F = 4.61$, 2 and 96 df, $p < .05$). Inspection of Table 1 shows clearly, however, that most of the variance is due to the large difference between the Control and Insult groups in the Track Film-Kirk condition. In three of the four columns of Table 1, nevertheless, the results are in the anticipated direction, with insulted subjects reporting more anger than frustrated ones, who in turn were more angry than controls.

Intensity and Duration of Shocks. The median shock intensity delivered by each subject for the 12 shock trials was calculated. The median was preferred to the mean as a measure of central tendency because several of the subjects gave a few shocks which were either extremely high or extremely low and thus falsely inflated or deflated group means. The mean of the medians for the 9 subjects in each condition was then obtained.

The analysis of variance of the data on shock intensity is reported in Table 2. This analysis shows that the Film $\times$ Treat-

TABLE 2: *Analysis of Variance for Shock Intensity Data*

Source	df	MS	F	P
1. Film	1	19.97	13.31	.005
2. Name	1	2.78	1.85	
3. Treatment	2	43.66	29.11	.001
4. 1 × 2	1	2.68	1.79	
5. 1 × 3	2	5.62	3.75	.05
6. 2 × 3	2	6.00	4.00	.05
7. 1 × 2 × 3	2	1.78	1.19	
8. Error	96	1.50		
9. Total	107			

ment interaction was significant (F = 3.75, 2 and 96 df, p < .05). Table 3 gives the group means involved in this interaction, along with the results of the Duncan test of differences among the means. The multiple-range tests reveal that in the Track

TABLE 3: *Mean Intensity of Shocks in the Treatment-by-Film Interaction*

Treatment	Boxing Film	Track Film
Control	2.84_c	3.18_c
Task Frustration	4.16_b	3.44_{bc}
Insult	5.80_a	4.11_b

Means having different subscripts are significantly different from each other at the .05 level of confidence by a Duncan Multiple Range Test. N = 18 in each condition.

Film condition only the Insult group gave significantly more intense shocks than the Control group. However, in the Boxing Film condition, both arousal treatments led to significantly more intense shocks than those given in the Control group. Insult resulted in the administration of stronger shocks than did task frustration, and task frustration led to the giving of stronger shocks than did the neutral behavior. Thus, while insult aroused the greatest degree of aggressive behavior, task frustration also created a readiness for aggression. The socially proper aggression these subjects then witnessed presumably lowered their inhibitions against this form of behavior. The subjects in the Track Film condition, on the other hand, did not receive the inhibition-lowering information, and an extreme provocation was required before these men would commit overt aggressive acts.

But did the witnessed violence do more than lower inhibitions generally? Further analysis of the shock intensity data reveals that the boxing film had effects other than the simple general reduction of inhibitions against aggression. Previous studies have shown that the boxing film produced a specific tendency in insulted subjects: to attack people associated with the victim of the witnessed aggression (Geen and Berkowitz, 1966; Berkowitz and Geen, 1966, 1967). On the basis of these findings, then, the confederate in the present study should receive more intense shocks when his name was "Kirk" rather than "Bob." More than this, we also ask whether this predicted greater volume of aggression against the high-cue target would arise only when the subject is insulted (the arousal treatment employed in the earlier studies), or whether it would also occur when the subject is frustrated (or is the recipient of the indirect blow to his self-esteem). Table 4 presents the data relevant to this question.

Looking at Table 4, there are no reliable differences among any of the four Control groups; the intensity of the electrical attacks was not greatly affected by the target's name or the nature of the film witnessed when the subjects were not emotionally aroused. As expected, the strongest aggression in the experiment was exhibited by the insulted men shown the boxing film who had an opportunity to attack a person with the same name as the film victim. However, this group was not significantly different from the Insult-Boxing Film-Bob group, and both of these insult-boxing film conditions differed reliably from the two nonaggressive film conditions. The task frustration led to a significantly weaker attack than the insult treatment, but only in the Boxing Film and not in the Track Film condition, possibly because a few of the men in the Frustrated-Track Film-Bob group were unusually responsive. In general, however, after the task frustration as after the insult, the most intense aggression was directed against the person having the same name as the victim of the observed aggression. While the Frustrated-Boxing Film-Kirk subjects did not differ significantly from the Bob subjects receiving the same arousal and film treatment, only the former, who had the presumably high-cue target, were significantly different from the Control-Boxing Film conditions. All in all, then, we have at least suggestive evidence here for our theoretical analysis; the task frustration led to stronger aggression than that displayed by a nonaroused group when (1) the thwarted men were given inhibition-lowering information and (2) were then provided with an opportunity to attack a person having high-cue value for aggression because of his name-mediated connection with the victim of the observed aggression.

The significant Name $\times$ Treatment interaction is difficult to interpret. The name "Kirk" might have an aggressive cue value

TABLE 4: *Intensity of Shocks Delivered by Subjects*

| Treatment | Boxing Film | | Track Film | |
	KIRK	BOB	KIRK	BOB
Control	3.07_{de}	2.60_e	3.34_{cde}	3.01_{de}
Task Frustration	4.49_{bc}	3.84_{cde}	3.91_{cd}	2.98_{de}
Insult	6.20_a	5.41_{ab}	3.99_{cd}	4.23_{cd}

Means having different subscripts are significantly different from each other at the .05 level of confidence by a Duncan Multiple Range Test. N = 9 in each condition.

in itself, leading to greater attacks on Kirk than Bob when the men were frustrated. Since this effect has not been observed in other experiments carried out in this laboratory, and did not arise in the Insult condition of this experiment, the present finding of high intensity shocks to Kirk in the Frustrated-Track Film group may well be only a chance occurrence.

The total duration of all 12 shocks delivered by the subject was noted, and from this an average duration was calculated. Analysis of these results indicated no significant effects. Generally, as we have always found, the best results are obtained with aggressive responses the subjects are set to make, whether shock number or shock intensity.

DISCUSSION

If the findings regarding the attacks upon the high-cue target under task frustration are reliable, we would have an easy explanation for the relationship between frustration and aggression: (1) The frustration produces a general arousal or drive state which is capable of energizing whatever response tendencies are elicited in the situation. (2) The highly salient aggressive cues evoke aggressive responses which are strongly energized by the arousal state. (3) The high arousal also results in a decreased responsivity to the peripheral cues in the situation (cf. Easterbrook, 1959) so that there is a temporary lessening of some possible interferences with the aggressive reaction. Any arousal state, regardless of its origin, could conceivably have these effects. However, to reinterpret the well-known research by Schachter (1964), the individual's cognitions regarding the origin of his emotion might also intervene, by inhibiting some actions but not others and by establishing appropriate cues in the environment.

There is also another possibility, however. The arousal state and eliciting cue could function in the manner just described, but certain types of arousal might still have specific consequences lacking in other kinds of states. There may well be a general activation common to all arousal states, but on top of this there may also be some specific components unique to certain states. (This, of course, is the type of observation Hull had made in his discussion of general and specific drives.) As an example, Roberts and Kiess (cited in Berkowitz, 1965a, p. 320) have demonstrated that electrical stimulation of the hypothalamus of cats did not create a general arousal state which merely intensified whatever response sequence happened to be under way at the time. If the cats were eating when the stimulation was turned on, they would turn to attack a nearby rat rather than consume their food with increased vigor. Berkowitz has observed (1965a, pp. 320–321): "This stimulation at least had a somewhat selective rather than general effect, and it may be that other types of arousal also increase the probability of certain response classes rather than making all actions equally likely."

Some critics of the frustration-aggression hypothesis, of course, have also taken a specificity position. They argue that only certain kinds of emotion-provoking situations generate aggression rather than all frustrations. Thus, Buss (1961, 1966) has maintained that only attacks produce aggressive reactions, while other writers (cf. Berkowitz, 1962) have said the specific determinant of aggression is a threat to the individual's ego or self-esteem. Advocates of this point of view could readily interpret the present task frustration as such a blow to the ego: the confederate completed his task while the subject was unable to do so, and therefore, indirectly deflated the subject's self-esteem. Additional research obviously is necessary before we can say unequivocally that any arousal situation is capable of producing the aggressive predisposition observed in this study.

REFERENCES

Bandura, A., Dorothea Ross, and Sheila A. Ross. Transmission of aggression through imitation of aggressive models. 63, *Journal of Abnormal and Social Psychology*, 1961, 575–582.

Bandura, A., Dorothea Ross, and Sheila A. Ross. Imitation of film-mediated aggressive models. 66, *Journal of Abnormal and Social Psychology*, 1963, 3–11.

Bandura, A., and R. H. Walters. *Social Learning and Personality Development*. New York: Holt, Rinehart & Winston, 1963.

Berkowitz, L. *Aggression: A Social Psychological Analysis*. New York: McGraw-Hill, 1962.

Berkowitz, L. Aggressive cues in aggressive behavior and hostility catharsis. 71, *Psychological Review*, 1964, 104–122.

Berkowitz, L. The concept of aggressive drive: Some additional considerations. In L. Berkowitz (ed.), *Advances in Experimental Social Psychology*, Vol. 2. New York: Academic Press, 1965a, pp. 301–329.

Berkowitz, L. Some aspects of observed aggression. 2, *Journal of Personality and Social Psychology*, 1965b, 359–369.

Berkowitz, L., R. Corwin, and R. Hieronimus. Film violence and subsequent aggressive tendencies. 27, *Public Opinion Quarterly*, 1963, 217–229.

Berkowitz, L., and R. G. Geen. Film violence and the cue properties of available targets. 3, *Journal of Personality and Social Psychology*, 1966, 525–530.

Berkowitz, L., and R. G. Geen. The stimulus qualities of the target of aggression: A further study. *Journal of Personality and Social Psychology*, 5, 1967, 364–368.

Berkowitz, L., and E. Rawlings. Effects of film violence on inhibitions against subsequent aggression. 66, *Journal of Abnormal and Social Psychology*, 1963, 405–412.

Buss, A. *The Psychology of Aggression*. New York: Wiley, 1961.

Buss, A. H. Instrumentality of aggression, feedback and frustration as determinants of physical aggression. 3, *Journal of Personality and Social Psychology*, 1966, 153–162.

Geen, R. G., and L. Berkowitz. Name-mediated aggressive cue properties. 34, *Journal of Personality*, 1966, 456–465.

Lovaas, O. I. Effect of exposure to symbolic aggression on aggressive behavior. 32, *Child Development*, 1961, 37–44.

Schachter, S. The interaction of cognitive and physiological determinants of emotional state. In L. Berkowitz (ed.), *Advances in Experimental Social Psychology*, Vol. 1. New York: Academic Press, 1964.

Walters, R. H., E. L. Thomas, and C. W. Acker. Enhancement of punitive behavior by audio-visual displays. 136, *Science*, 1962, 872–873.

Wheeler, L., and A. A. Caggiula. The contagion of aggression. 2, *Journal of Experimental Social Psychology*, 1966, 1–10.

NOTES

1. See Geen and Berkowitz (1966) for the complete questionnaire.
2. See Berkowitz and Geen (1967) for a complete description of the name manipulation.
3. The four items on the final questionnaire served as a secondary aggression measure. Each of the four scales was preceded by the qualification, "From what you now know about the other subject in this experiment . . ." followed by the specific question. On these items the subject responded along a continuum from VERY MUCH (1) to NOT AT ALL (7). Item 1 asked, "How much would you like to serve in another experiment with him?" A significant main effect due to the arousal treatment was obtained ($F = 5.07$, 2 and 96 df, $p < .05$), but the findings do not parallel those obtained with shock intensity. There was also a significant main effect for the arousal treatments on the item, "How much would you like to have him for a personal friend?" ($F = 12.43$, 2 and 96 df, $p < .001$). But the results with this measure also do not follow the shock findings. The insulted men expressed more intense hostility than did any of the other subjects, although the differences between the Task Frustration and Control conditions and the target's name did not have any effect on the attacks he received.

There are any number of possible explanations for the discrepancy between shock and questionnaire results. Most obviously, giving the shocks could have affected the following verbal statements in some unspecifiable manner. There was no simple catharsis operating here. The insulted men, who had delivered the most intense shocks, subsequently expressed the greatest rejection of the confederate as a friend. Rather than producing an emotional purge, the physical attacks could have led to inhibitions against further aggression in some cases and, perhaps, to a self-justifying strong verbal condemnation of the confederate in other instances.

8 : *Toward a Theory of Revolution*

JAMES C. DAVIES

In exhorting proletarians of all nations to unite in revolution because they had nothing to lose but their chains, Marx and Engels most succinctly presented that theory of revolution which is recognized as their brain child. But this most famed thesis, that progressive degradation of the industrial working class would finally reach the point of despair and inevitable revolt, is not the only one that Marx fathered. In at least one essay he gave life to a quite antithetical idea. He described, as a precondition of widespread unrest, not progressive degradation of the proletariat but rather an improvement in workers' economic conditions which did not keep pace with the growing welfare of capitalists and therefore produced social tension.

From *American Sociological Review*, vol. 27, 1962, pp. 5–8, 15–18.

Several people have made perceptive suggestions and generous comments on an earlier version of this paper. I wish particularly to thank Seymour Martin Lipset, Lucian W. Pye, John H. Schaar, Paul Seabury, and Dwight Waldo.

A noticeable increase in wages presupposes a rapid growth of productive capital. The rapid growth of productive capital brings about an equally rapid growth of wealth, luxury, social wants, social enjoyments. Thus, although the enjoyments of the workers have risen, the social satisfaction that they give has fallen in comparison with the increased enjoyments of the capitalist, which are inaccessible to the worker, in comparison with the state of development of society in general. Our desires and pleasures spring from society; we measure them, therefore, by society and not by the objects which serve for their satisfaction. Because they are of a social nature, they are of a relative nature.[1]

Marx's qualifications here of his more frequent belief that degradation produces revolution is expressed as the main thesis by de Tocqueville in his study of the French Revolution. After a long review of economic and social decline in the seventeenth century and dynamic growth in the eighteenth, de Tocqueville concludes:

So it would appear that the French found their condition the more unsupportable in proportion to its improvement. . . . Revolutions are not always brought about by a gradual decline from bad to worse. Nations that have endured patiently and almost unconsciously the most overwhelming oppression often burst into rebellion against the yoke the moment it begins to grow lighter. The regime which is destroyed by a revolution is almost always an improvement on its immediate predecessor. . . . Evils which are patiently endured when they seem inevitable become intolerable when once the idea of escape from them is suggested.[2]

On the basis of de Tocqueville and Marx, we can choose one of these ideas or the other, which makes it hard to decide just when revolutions are more likely to occur—when there has been social and economic progress or when there has been regress. It appears that both ideas have explanatory and possibly predictive value, if they are juxtaposed and put in the proper time sequence.

Revolutions are most likely to occur when a prolonged period of objective economic and social development is followed by a short period of sharp reversal.[3] The all-important effect on the minds of people in a particular society is to produce, during the former period, an expectation of continued ability to satisfy needs—which continue to rise—and, during the latter, a mental state of anxiety and frustration when manifest reality breaks away from anticipated reality. The actual state of socio-economic development is less significant than the expectation that past progress, now blocked, can and must continue in the future.

Political stability and instability are ultimately dependent on a state of mind, a mood, in a society. Satisfied or apathetic people who are poor in goods, status, and power can remain politically quiet and their opposites can revolt, just as, correlatively and more probably, dissatisfied poor can revolt and satisfied rich oppose revolution. It is the dissatisfied state of mind rather than the tangible provision of "adequate" or "inadequate" supplies of food, equality, or liberty which produces the revolution. In actuality, there must be a joining of forces between dissatisfied, frustrated people who differ in their degree of objective, tangible welfare and status. Well-fed, well-educated, high-status individuals who rebel in the face of apathy among the objectively deprived can accomplish at most a coup d'état. The objectively deprived, when faced with solid opposition of people of wealth, status, and power, will be smashed in their rebellion as were peasants and Anabaptists by German noblemen in 1525 and East Germans by the communist elite in 1953.

Before appraising this general notion in light of a series of revolutions, a word is in order as to why revolutions ordinarily do not occur when a society is generally impoverished—when, as de Tocqueville put it, evils that seem inevitable are patiently endured. They are endured in the extreme case because the physical and mental energies of people are totally employed in the process of merely staying alive. The Minnesota starvation studies conducted during World War II[4] indicate clearly the constant preoccupation of very hungry individuals with fantasies and thoughts of food. In extremis, as the Minnesota research poignantly demonstrates, the individual withdraws into a life of his own, withdraws from society, withdraws from any significant kind of activity unrelated to staying alive. Reports of behavior in Nazi concentration camps indicate the same preoccupation.[5] In less extreme and barbarous circumstances, where minimal survival is possible but little more, the preoccupation of individuals with staying alive is only mitigated. Social action takes place for the most part on a local, face-to-face basis. In such circumstances the family is a—perhaps the major —solidary unit[6] and even the local community exists primarily to the extent families need to act together to secure their separate survival. Such was life on the American frontier in the seventeenth through nineteenth centuries. In very much attenuated form, but with a substantial degree of social isolation persisting, such evidently is rural life even today. This is clearly related to a relatively low level of political participation in elections.[7] As Zawadzki and Lazarsfeld have indicated,[8] preoccupation with physical survival, even in industrial areas, is a force strongly militating against the establishment of the community-sense and consensus on joint political action which are necessary to induce a revolutionary state of mind. Far from making people into revolutionaries, enduring poverty makes for concern with one's solitary self or solitary family at best and resignation or mute despair at worst. When it is a choice between losing their chains or their lives, people will mostly choose to keep their chains, a fact which Marx seems to have overlooked.[9]

It is when the chains have been loosened somewhat, so that they can be cast off without a high probability of losing life, that people are put in a condition of proto-rebelliousness. I use the term proto-rebelliousness because the mood of discontent may be dissipated before a violent outbreak occurs. The causes for such dissipation may be natural or social (including economic and political). A bad crop year that threatens a return to chronic hunger may be succeeded by a year of natural abundance. Recovery from sharp economic dislocation may take the steam from the boiler of rebellion.[10] The slow, grudging grant of reforms, which has been the political history of England since at least the Industrial Revolution, may effectively and continuously prevent the degree of frustration that produces revolt.

A revolutionary state of mind requires the continued, even habitual but dynamic expectation of greater opportunity to satisfy basic needs, which may range from merely physical (food, clothing, shelter, health, and safety from bodily harm) to social (the affectional ties of family and friends) to the need for equal dignity and justice. But the necessary additional ingredient is a persistent, unrelenting threat to the satisfaction of these needs: not a threat which actually returns people to a state of sheer survival but which puts them in the mental state where they believe they will not be able to satisfy one or more basic needs. Although physical deprivation in some degree may be threatened on the eve of all revolutions, it need not be the prime factor, as it surely was not in the American Revolution of 1775. The crucial factor is the vague or specific fear that ground gained over a long period of time will be quickly lost. This fear does not generate if there is continued opportunity to satisfy continually emerging needs; it generates when the existing government suppresses or is blamed for suppressing such opportunity.

Three rebellions or revolutions are given considerable attention in the original article: Dorr's Rebellion of 1842, the Russian Revolution of 1917, and the Egyptian Revolution of 1952. Brief mention is then made of several other major civil disturbances, all of which appear to fit the J-curve pattern.[11]

No claim is made that all rebellions follow the pattern, but just that the ones here presented do. All of these are "progressive" revolutions in behalf of greater equality and liberty. The question is open whether the pattern occurs in such markedly retrogressive revolutions as Nazism in Germany or the 1861 Southern rebellion in the United States. It will surely be necessary to examine other progressive revolutions before one can judge how universal the J-curve is. And it will be necessary, in the interests of scientific validation, to examine cases of serious civil disturbance that fell short of producing profound revolution—such as the Sepoy Rebellion of 1857 in India, the Pullman Strike of 1894 in America, the Boxer Rebellion of 1900 in China, and the Great Depression of the 1920s and 1930s as it was experienced in Austria, France, Great Britain, and the United States. The explanation for such stillborn rebellions—for revolutions that might have occurred—is inevitably more complicated than for those that come to term in the "normal" course of political gestation. . . .

The American Revolution itself fits the J-curve and deserves more than the brief mention here given. Again prolonged economic growth and political autonomy produced continually rising expectations. They became acutely frustrated when, following the French and Indian War (which had cost England so much and the colonies so little), England began a series of largely economic regulations having the same purpose as those directed against New York in the preceding century. From the 1763 Proclamation (closing to settlement land west of the Appalachians) to the Coercive Acts of April 1774 (which among other things, in response to the December 1773 Boston Tea Party, closed tight the port of Boston), Americans were beset with unaccustomed manifestations of British power and began to resist forcibly in 1775, on the Lexington-Concord road. A significant decline in trade with England in 1772[12] may have hastened the maturation of colonial rebelliousness.

The curve also fits the French Revolution, which again merits more mention than space here permits. Growing rural prosperity, marked by steadily rising land values in the eighteenth century, had progressed to the point where a third of French land was owned by peasant proprietors. There were the beginnings of large-scale manufacture in the factory system. Constant pressure by the bourgeoisie against the state for reforms was met with considerable hostility by a government already shifting from its old landed-aristocratic and clerical base to the growing middle class. Counter to these trends, which would per se avoid revolution, was the feudal reaction of the mid-eighteenth century, in which the dying nobility sought in numerous nagging ways to retain and reactivate its perquisites against a resentful peasantry and importunate bourgeoisie.

But expectations apparently continued rising until the growing opportunities and prosperity rather abruptly halted, about 1787. The fiscal crisis of the government is well known, much of it a consequence of a 1.5 billion livre deficit following intervention against Britain in the American war of independence. The threat to tax the nobility severely—after its virtual tax immunity—and the bourgeoisie more severely may indeed be said to have precipitated the revolution. But less well-known is the fact that 1787 was a bad harvest year and 1788 even worse; that by July 1789 bread prices were higher than they had been in over 70 years; that an ill-timed trade treaty with England depressed the prices of French textiles; that a concurrent bumper grape crop depressed wine prices—all with the result of making desperate the plight of the large segment of the population now dependent on other producers for food. They had little money to buy even less bread. Nobles and bourgeoisie were alienated from the government by the threat of taxation; workers and some peasants by the threat of starvation. A long period of halting but real progress for virtually all segments of the population was now abruptly ended in consequence of the government's efforts to meet its deficit and of economic crisis resulting from poor crops and poor tariff policy.[13]

The draft riots that turned the city of New York upside down for five days in July 1863 also follow the J-curve. This severe local disturbance began when conscription threatened the lives and fortunes of workingmen whose enjoyment of wartime prosperity was now frustrated not only by military service (which could be avoided by paying $300 or furnishing a substitute—neither means being available to poor people) but also by inflation.[14]

Even the riots in Nyasaland, in February and March 1959, appear to follow the pattern of a period of frustration after expectations and satisfactions have risen. Nyasaland workers who had enjoyed the high wages they were paid during the construction of the Kariba dam in Rhodesia returned to their homes and to unemployment, or to jobs paying $5 per month at a time when $15 was considered a bare minimum wage.[15]

One negative case—of a revolution that did not occur—is the Depression of the 1930s in the United States. It was severe enough, at least on economic grounds, to have produced a revolution. Total national private production income in 1932 reverted to what it had been in 1916. Farm income in the same year was as low as in 1900; manufacturing as low as in 1913. Construction had not been as low since 1908. Mining and quarrying were back at the 1909 level.[16] For much of the population, two decades of economic progress had been wiped out. There were more than sporadic demonstrations by the unemployed, hunger marchers, and veterans. In New York City, at least 29 people died of starvation. Poor people could vividly contrast their own past condition with the present—and their own present condition with that of those who were not seriously suffering. There were clearly audible rumbles of revolt. Why, then, no revolution?

Several forces worked strongly against it. Among the most depressed, the mood was one of apathy and despair, like that observed in Austria by Zawadzki and Lazarsfeld. It was not until the 1936 election that there was an increased turnout in the national election. The great majority of the public shared a set of values which since 1776 had been official dogma—not the dissident program of an alienated intelligentsia. People by and large were in agreement, whether or not they had succeeded economically, in a belief in individual hard work, self-reliance, and the promise of success. (Among workers, this nonclass orientation had greatly impeded the establishment of trade unions, for example.) Those least hit by the Depression—the upper-middle-class businessmen, clergymen, lawyers, and intellectuals—remained rather solidly committed not only to equalitarian values and to the established economic system but also to constitutional processes. There was no such widespread or profound alienation as that which had cracked the loyalty of the nobility, clergy, bourgeoisie, armed forces, and intelligentsia in Russia. And the national political leadership that emerged had constitutionalism almost bred in its bones. The major threat to constitutionalism came in Louisiana; this leadership was unable to capture a national party organization, in part because Huey Long's arbitrariness and demagogy were mistrusted.

The major reason that revolution did not nonetheless develop probably remains the vigor with which the national government attacked the Depression in 1933, when it became no longer possible to blame the government. The ambivalent popular hostility to the business community was contained by both the action of government against the Depression and the government's practice of publicly and successfully eliciting the cooperation of businessmen during the crucial months of 1933. A failure then of cooperation could have intensified rather than lessened popular hostility to business. There was no longer an economic or a political class that could be the object of widespread intense hatred because of its indifference or hostility to the downtrodden. Had Roosevelt adopted a demagogic stance in the 1932 campaign and gained the loyalty to himself personally of the Army and the FBI, there might have been a Nazi-type "revolution," with a potpourri of equalitarian reform, nationalism, imperialism, and domestic scapegoats. Because of a conservatism in America stemming from strong and long attachment to a value system shared by all classes, an anticapitalist, leftist revolution in the 1930s is very difficult to imagine.

SOME CONCLUSIONS

The notion that revolutions need both a period of rising expectations and a succeeding period in which they are frustrated qualifies substantially the main Marxian notion that revolutions occur after progressive degradation and the de Tocqueville notion that they occur when conditions are improving. By putting de Tocqueville before Marx but without abandoning either theory, we are better able to plot the antecedents of at least the disturbances here described.

Half of the general, if not common, sense of this revised notion lies in the utter improbability of a revolution occurring in a society where there is the continued, unimpeded opportunity to satisfy new needs, new hopes, new expectations. Would Dorr's Rebellion have become such if the established electorate and government had readily acceded to the suffrage demands of the unpropertied? Would the Russian Revolution have taken place if the Tsarist autocracy had, quite out of character, truly granted the popular demands for constitutional democracy in 1905? Would the Cairo riots of January 1952 and the subsequent coup actually have occurred if Britain had departed from Egypt and if the Egyptian monarchy had established an equitable tax system and in other ways alleviated the poverty of urban masses and the shame of the military?

The other half of the sense of the notion has to do with the improbability of revolution taking place where there has been no hope, no period in which expectations have risen. Such a stability of expectations presupposes a static state of human aspirations that sometimes exists but is rare. Stability of expectations is not a stable social condition. Such was the case of American Indians (at least from our perspective) and perhaps Africans before white men with Bibles, guns, and other goods interrupted the stability of African society. Egypt was in such a condition, vis-à-vis modern aspirations, before Europe became interested in building a canal. Such stasis was the case in Nazi concentration camps, where conformism reached the point of inmates cooperating with guards even when the inmates were told to lie down so that they could be shot.[17] But in the latter case there was a society with externally induced complete despair, and even in these camps there were occasional rebellions of sheer desperation. It is of course true that in a society less regimented than concentration camps, the rise of expectations can be frustrated successfully, thereby defeating rebellion just as the satisfaction of expectations does. This, however, requires the uninhibited exercise of brute force as it was used in suppressing the Hungarian rebellion of 1956. Failing the continued ability and persistent will of a ruling power to use such force, there appears to be no sure way to avoid revolution short of an effective, affirmative, and continuous response on the part of established governments to the almost continuously emerging needs of the governed.

NOTES

1. The *Communist Manifesto* of 1848 evidently antedates the opposing idea by about a year. See Edmund Wilson, *To the Finland Station* (Anchor Books edition), New York: Doubleday, n.d., p. 157; Lewis S. Feuer, *Karl Marx and Friedrich Engels: Basic Writings on Politics and Philosophy*, New York: Doubleday, 1959, p. 1. The above quotation is from Karl Marx and Frederick Engels, "Wage Labour and Capital," *Selected Works in Two Volumes*, Moscow: Foreign Languages Publishing House, 1955, Vol. I, p. 94.
2. A. de Tocqueville, *The Old Regime and the French Revolution* (trans. by John Bonner), New York: Harper, 1856, p. 214. The Stuart Gilbert translation, Garden City: Doubleday, 1955, pp. 176–177, gives a somewhat less pungent version of the same comment. *L'Ancien régime* was first published in 1856.
3. Revolutions are here defined as violent civil disturbances that cause the displacement of one ruling group by another that has a broader popular basis for support.
4. The full report is Ancel Keys et al., *The Biology of Human Starvation*, Minneapolis: University of Minnesota Press, 1950. See J. Brozek, "Semi-starvation and Nutritional Rehabilitation," *Journal of Clinical Nutrition*, 1 (January 1953), 107–118, for a brief analysis.
5. E. A. Cohen, *Human Behavior in the Concentration Camp*, New York: Norton, 1953, pp. 123–125, 131–140.
6. For community life in such poverty, in Mezzogiorno, Italy, see E. C. Banfield, *The Moral Basis of a Backward Society*, New York: The Free Press, 1958. The author emphasizes that the nuclear family is a solidary, consensual, moral unit (see p. 85) but even within it, consensus appears to break down, in outbreaks of pure, individual amorality—notably between parents and children (see p. 117).
7. See Angus Campbell *et al.*, *The American Voter*, New York: Wiley, 1960, Chapter 15, "Agrarian Political Behavior."

8. B. Zawadzki and P. F. Lazarsfeld, "The Psychological Consequences of Unemployment," *Journal of Social Psychology*, 6 (May 1935), 224–251.

9. A remarkable and awesome exception to this phenomenon occurred occasionally in some Nazi concentration camps, e.g., in a Buchenwald revolt against capricious rule by criminal prisoners. During this revolt, 100 criminal prisoners were killed by political prisoners. See Cohen, *op. cit.*, p. 200.

10. See W. W. Rostow, "Business Cycles, Harvests, and Politics: 1790–1850," *Journal of Economic History*, 1 (November 1941), 206–221, for the relation between economic fluctuation and the activities of the Chartists in the 1830s and 1840s.

11. This curve is of course not to be confused with its prior and altogether different use by Floyd Allport in his study of social conformity. See F. H. Allport, "The J-Curve Hypothesis of Conforming Behavior," *Journal of Social Psychology*, 5 (May, 1934), 141–183, reprinted in T. H. Newcomb and E. L. Hartley, *Readings in Social Psychology*, New York: Holt, 1947, pp. 55–67.

12. See U.S. Bureau of the Census, *Historical Statistics of the United States, Colonial Times to 1957*, Washington, D.C.: GPO, 1960, p. 757.

13. See G. Lefebvre, *The Coming of the French Revolution*, Princeton: Princeton University Press, 1947, pp. 101–109, 145–148, 196. G. Le Bon, *The Psychology of Revolution*, New York: Putnam's, 1913, p. 143.

14. The account by Irving Werstein, *July 1863*, New York: Messner, 1957, is journalistic but to my knowledge the fullest yet available.

15. E. S. Munger, "The Tragedy of Nyasaland," American Universities Field Staff Reports Service, Vol. 7, No. 4 (August 1, 1959), p. 9.

16. See U.S. Bureau of the Census, *Historical Statistics of the United States: 1789–1945*, Washington, D.C.: GPO, 1949, p. 14.

17. Eugen Kogon, *The Theory and Practice of Hell*, New York: Farrar, Straus, 1950, pp. 284–286.

Name Index

131

Subject Index